GOD
HAS
SPOKEN
AGAIN

A BOOK OF THE
NEW MESSAGE
FROM GOD

GOD
HAS
SPOKEN
AGAIN

AS REVEALED TO

Marshall Vian Summers

GOD
HAS
SPOKEN
AGAIN

Edited by Darlene Mitchell
Cover and interior: Designed by Reed Summers

ISBN: 978-1-942293-00-2
NKL POD Version 4.1
Library of Congress Control Number: 2014919201

Publisher's Cataloging-in-Publication
(Provided by Quality Books, Inc.)

Summers, Marshall Vian.
   God has spoken again / as revealed
to Marshall Vian Summers.
   pages cm
   LCCN 2014919201
   ISBN 978-1-942293-00-2 (POD)
   ISBN 978-1-942293-01-9 (ebook)

   1. Society for the New Message--Doctrines.
   2. Spiritual life--Society for the New Message.
   I. Society for the New Message.
   II. Title.
      BP605.S58S8195 2014   299'.93
                                QBI14-600186

God Has Spoken Again is a book of the New Message from God and is published by New Knowledge Library, the publishing imprint of The Society for the New Message. The Society is a religious non-profit organization dedicated to presenting and teaching a New Message for humanity. The books of New Knowledge Library can be ordered at www.newknowledgelibrary.org, your local bookstore and at many other online retailers.

The New Message is being studied in 20 languages in over 92 countries. *God Has Spoken Again* has been translated into 18 languages by a dedicated group of volunteer student translators from around the world. These translations will all be available online at www.newmessage.org.

The Society for the New Message
P.O. Box 1724   Boulder, CO 80306-1724
(303) 938-8401   (800) 938-3891
011 303 938 84 01 (International)   (303) 938-1214 (fax)
newmessage.org newknowledgelibrary.org
email: society@newmessage.org

We shall speak of God, the Higher Authority.

The Higher Authority is speaking to you now,
speaking through the Angelic Presence,
speaking to a part of you that is the very center
and source of your Being.

The Higher Authority has a Message for the world
and for each person in the world.

The Higher Authority is calling to you, calling to you down
through the Ancient Corridors of your mind,
calling to you beyond your beliefs and your preoccupations.

For God has spoken again and
the Word and the Sound are in the world.

From *God Has Spoken Again*
Chapter 3: The Engagement

GOD
HAS
SPOKEN
AGAIN

TABLE OF CONTENTS

Introduction i

CHAPTER 1   The Proclamation 1

CHAPTER 2   The Recitation 5

CHAPTER 3   The Engagement 17

CHAPTER 4   God Has Spoken Again 25

CHAPTER 5   The Seal of the Prophets 35

CHAPTER 6   The Mission of the Messenger 45

CHAPTER 7   The Initiation 59

CHAPTER 8   The Blessing..71

CHAPTER 9   Living at a Time of Revelation 83

CHAPTER 10   The Assembly..95

CHAPTER 11   God's New Message for the World.........................107

CHAPTER 12   God Is Moving Humanity in a New Direction..........115

CHAPTER 13   The World Must Receive God's New Message 123

CHAPTER 14   The Calling...135

Important Terms 147

The Messenger 153

The Voice of Revelation 155

About the Worldwide Community of the New Message 157

About The Society for the New Message 159

INTRODUCTION

This book contains the opening words of a New Message from God. In the pages that follow, God is speaking to humanity anew, providing a warning, a blessing and a preparation for the great change that is coming to the world.

God has spoken again at a time of great need and difficulty worldwide. This is a Divine answer to the growing crises of war, unrelenting climate change, religious conflict, and human suffering and deprivation now escalating around the world.

The New Message from God is a living communication from God to the heart of every man, woman and child on Earth. The Word and the Sound are in the world again. We are living at a time of Revelation.

The New Message from God has not entered the world through the existing religious authorities and institutions of today. It has not come to the leaders of religion or to those who garner fame and recognition.

Instead, God's New Message has entered the world as it has always done. It has come quietly, unlooked-for and unannounced, given to a humble man chosen and sent into the world for this one task, to be a Messenger for humanity at this great turning point.

Though it appears to be a book in the hand, *God Has Spoken Again* is something far greater. It is the beginning of a living communication from God to you. In the pages of this book, God's Presence calls to you and to all people, calling for you to awaken from the dream and the nightmare of living in Separation apart from your Source, calling down through the Ancient Corridors of your mind to the spiritual presence and power that live within you, waiting to be discovered.

It is this spiritual presence within you that will confirm the truth and authenticity of God's New Message. Here the mind may doubt and struggle with the gift and challenge of a New Revelation, but your heart will know. At this deeper level, you will not need convincing—the truth will be apparent to you.

Has God spoken again? Is this the Message you have been looking for? Read the words of Revelation in this book and at a deeper level you will know if it is real, honest and pure, even if it is different from what you may currently believe. It is this inner knowing and confirmation that can recall to you the depth and power of your connection to God.

What you hold in your hands is a book of Revelation. The words in this text are the direct communication from God, translated into human language by the Angelic Presence that oversees the world, and then spoken through their Messenger Marshall Vian Summers.

The New Message from God is the largest Revelation ever given to humanity, given now to a literate world of global communication and growing global awareness. It is not given for one tribe, one nation or one religion alone, but instead to reach the entire world, a world very different from the ancient world of the former Messengers. Never before has there been a Divine Revelation of this depth and magnitude, given by God to all people of the world, in the lifetime of the Messenger.

At the center of the New Message from God is the original Voice of Revelation, which has spoken every word of every book of the New Message. Never before has the Voice of Revelation, the Voice that spoke to the Messengers and Prophets of the past, been recorded in its original purity and made available to each person to hear and to experience for themselves. In this way, the Word and the Sound are in the world.

In this remarkable process of spoken Revelation, the Presence of God communicates beyond words to the Angelic Assembly that oversees the world. The Assembly then translates this communication into human language and speaks all as one through their Messenger, whose voice becomes the vehicle for this greater Voice—the Voice of Revelation.

INTRODUCTION

The words of this Voice were recorded in audio form, transcribed and are now made available in the texts and audio recordings of the New Message. In this way, the purity of God's original Message is preserved and given to all people in the world.

The Messenger has walked a long and difficult road to bring the New Message from God into the world. The process of Revelation began in 1982 and continues to this day.

At this time, the Messenger is engaged in compiling over three decades of spoken Revelation into a final and complete text form. The New Message will ultimately be contained in six volumes and possibly more. Each volume will contain two or more books, and each book will be organized into chapters and verses. Therefore, the New Message from God will be structured in the following way: Volume > Book > Chapter > Verse.

God Has Spoken Again is Book 1 contained in Volume 1 of the New Message from God. Therefore, this text contains the opening words of God's New Message and stands as the first book in the growing library of the New Revelation.

God Has Spoken Again contains 14 individual revelations, compiled into this book by the Messenger. With this, the reader should understand that this book is not a series of chapters delivered in sequence, but instead is a compilation of individual spoken revelations given at different times and places.

In order to bring this spoken communication into written form, slight textual and grammatical adjustments were made by the Messenger. This was requested of him by the Angelic Assembly to aid the understanding of the reader and to convey the Message according to the grammatical standards of the written English language.

In some instances, the Messenger has inserted a word not originally spoken in the Revelation. When present, this inserted word will be found [in brackets.] Consider these bracketed insertions as direct clarifications by the Messenger, placed in the text by him alone in order to ensure that ambiguities in the spoken communication do not cause confusion or incorrect interpretations of the text.

In some cases, the Messenger has removed a word to aid the readability of the text. This was usually done in the case of certain conjunctions (such as the words *and, but*) that made the text awkward or grammatically incorrect.

The Messenger alone has made these slight changes and only to convey the original spoken communication with the greatest clarity possible. None of the original meaning or intention of the communication has been altered.

The text of this book has been structured by the Messenger into verse. Each verse roughly signals the beginning or ending of a distinct topic or message point communicated by the Source.

The verse structure of the text allows the reader to access the richness of the content and those subtle messages that may otherwise be missed in longer paragraphs of text that convey multiple topics. In this way, each topic and idea communicated by the Source is given its own standing, allowing it to speak from the page directly to the reader. The Messenger has determined that structuring the text in verse is the most efficacious and faithful way of rendering the original spoken revelations of the New Message.

The rendering of this text is according to the Messenger's original will and intention. Here we are privileged to witness the process of compilation being undertaken by the Messenger, in his own time, by his own hands. This stands in contrast to the fact that the former great traditions were not put into written form by their Messengers, leaving the original Revelations vulnerable to alteration and corruption over time.

Here the Messenger seals in purity the texts of God's New Message and gives them to you, to the world and to all people in the future. Whether this book is opened today or 500 years from now,

God's original communication will speak from these pages with the same intimacy, purity and power as on the day it was spoken.

God Has Spoken Again is the beginning of a living communication from God to humanity. The chapters of this book are like breaths in that communication. Here, God is calling to humanity; calling across the world into every nation, culture and faith community; calling into the halls of government and religion; calling into the darkest places where inner suffering and physical deprivation are deepest; calling for the spiritual power of humanity to emerge and for humanity to unite and cooperate sufficiently to prepare for the great challenges ahead.

Remarkably you have found the New Message from God, or it has found you. It is no coincidence that this is the case. God is calling now across the world and this calling has found you.

Here opens the next chapter in the mystery of your life and of your presence in the world at this time. The door opens before you. You need only enter to begin.

As you enter more deeply into the Revelation, the impact on your life will grow, bringing a greater experience of clarity, inner certainty and true direction to your life. In time, your questions will be answered as you find growing freedom from self-doubt, inner conflict and the restraints of the past. This is the Power of Heaven speaking to you directly, revealing to you the greater life that you were always destined to live.

New Knowledge Library

CHAPTER 1

THE PROCLAMATION

As revealed to
Marshall Vian Summers
on July 7, 2006
in Boulder, Colorado

There is a New Message from God in the World. It has come from the Creator of all life.

It has been translated into human language and understanding through the Angelic Presence that oversees this world.

It continues the great series of transmissions from the Creator that have occurred over centuries and millennia.

It is a New Message for this time and the times to come.

It fulfills the former Messages that have been given to humanity, and yet it reveals things that have never been shown to humanity before. For humanity is now facing a grave and perilous set of challenges, both within the world and from beyond the world.

The New Message from God is here to alert, to empower and to prepare the human family—people from all nations and religious traditions, from all tribes, groups and orientations.

It has come at a time of great need, a time of great consequence. It is preparing people for things that have not even been recognized.

It is prophetic in alerting people to the Great Waves of change that are coming to the world and to humanity's position in the universe, especially regarding your contact with other races.

It calls upon the great spiritual presence within each person—the great endowment of Knowledge that has been given to the entire human family, which must now be cultivated, strengthened and brought forth.

It speaks to the great spiritual need of the individual—the need for purpose, meaning and direction.

It speaks to the great relationships that people can establish with one another, relationships representing their higher purpose in life.

It speaks to the needs of the world and the needs of the future. In so doing, it brings purpose and recognition, unity and cooperation, wisdom and strength to all who can receive it, who can learn it, who can follow its steps, who can contribute it to others and who can share its wisdom in service to other individuals, to families, to communities, to nations and to the whole world.

Receive this blessing. Learn of the New Message from God. Realize it will affirm all that is true within your current traditions, and it will speak to the deeper wisdom that you already possess. It will speak to your heart, even beyond your thoughts and beliefs and the thoughts and beliefs of your culture or your nation.

Receive this gift and learn of it patiently, taking the Steps to Knowledge, learning the wisdom from the Greater Community and recognizing the power of the One Spirituality of humanity in uniting humanity, in strengthening humanity and in preparing humanity to recognize and to navigate the difficult times ahead.

THE PROCLAMATION

Receive the New Message in its calling for the preservation and the strengthening of human freedom, cooperation and responsibility.

For without this New Message, humanity is facing a grave and precipitous decline.

It is facing the loss of its freedom and sovereignty in this world to other intervening forces from the universe around you.

Without this New Message, the human spirit will remain dormant, and people will live lives of desperation, competition and conflict.

It is the Creator's Will that humanity emerge into the Greater Community of life in the universe as a free and sovereign race—as a strong race, as a united race, as a race that is capable of maintaining its cultural diversity while honoring the deeper strength and purpose that will keep the world strong and keep the human family vital, active and creative, presenting a new opportunity for advancement in the future.

But to advance you must survive. You must survive the difficult times ahead, and you must survive competition from beyond the world regarding who will control this world and its destiny.

Each individual must recognize that they have a great opportunity to discover the deeper Knowledge that God has given them—the Knowledge which contains their purpose, their meaning and their direction and the criteria for all their meaningful relationships.

Therefore, there is a New Message from God for the individual, and there is a New Message from God for the entire world. It is here now.

It has taken a long time for the Messenger to receive it, for the Message is very great.

Honor then the one who has come to bring the New Message into the world.

He is a humble man. He has developed the wisdom necessary to undertake such a great role, and he has been sent into the world for this purpose.

Receive him. Understand him. Do not exalt him. He is not a god. He is a Messenger bringing the New Message from God into the world.

This is the time now. This is the great opportunity. This is the answer to people's prayers all around the world—prayers through every faith tradition, through every nation and culture, praying for wisdom, strength, unity, freedom and deliverance.

Receive this New Message now. It is come, and it is come at just the right time.

CHAPTER 2

THE RECITATION

*As revealed to
Marshall Vian Summers
on April 1, 2011
in Boulder, Colorado*

God has spoken again.

We are the ones to bring the Message. God's Will is presented through Us.

We are beyond your estimation, beyond your religious theories and your personal speculation.

For human imagination can only fabricate from what it experiences in the physical world. But reality exists beyond this—beyond the realm and the reach of the intellect.

This is the truth throughout the universe, the Greater Community of life in which you live.

We bring the Great Message for this era, born of the Creator of all the universes, for the protection of humanity, for the salvation of the world.

We are the ones whom you cannot understand. But We are the source and the medium of what humanity must recognize and do on its own behalf, what it must see, what it has not seen, what it must know, what it has not known, what it must do, which it has not done.

This is the Message for this era. This is the time of Revelation.

One has been sent into the world to receive the Revelation and to bring it into human awareness, a monumental task.

To receive the New Message is to receive the greatest Revelation that has ever been given to the human family.

To present it to the world is a monumental task, a task for the Messenger and for all who will assist him in bringing the Revelation everywhere it is needed.

It is needed everywhere, for humanity is facing great peril. It has sown the seeds of its own demise through the destruction and the degradation of its environment—its waters, its soil, its air—to the point where the world itself is beginning to change, a change that will bring great trial and tribulation to the world of people and to the human family.

Humanity is facing a universe of intelligent life. It will have to prepare for this now, for contact has begun—contact by those who see the opportunity to take advantage of a weak and conflicted humanity.

It is a time of great change and uncertainty, where foreign powers will seek to gain influence and where humanity will fall prey to its own ignorance, foolishness and indulgences.

The Message is too big to say in a sentence, but it will bring you closer to God and what God has sent you, as an individual, here to do in the world now, which is far different from what you believe and imagine today.

God has brought wisdom from the universe to prepare humanity for the universe.

God has brought the essence of spirituality in a pure form—unclouded by history and human manipulation, unfettered by human politics, will and corruption.

We bring the Steps to Knowledge so that you may know of the deeper mind that God has placed within you to guide you in an increasingly perilous world.

Great upheaval will now occur and is beginning to occur—natural disasters born of humanity's ignorance and overuse and misuse of the world.

It is a time of reckoning, a time of responsibility, a time to end foolishness and arrogance.

Only God knows what is coming.

And We have brought the Message—a Message of a thousand messages, a Message of a thousand teachings, a Message great enough to occupy you for the rest of your time, a Message great enough to redirect human effort, energy and awareness so that humanity may have a greater future than its past, so that humanity may survive the Great Waves of change and intervention and competition from the universe around you.

Hear this then, not with your ideas, your beliefs or your judgments, but with the deeper mind that God has given you to hear, to see, to know and to act with greater certainty.

Our words are not for speculation or debate. That is the indulgence of the foolish, who cannot hear and cannot see.

You are terrified of the Revelation, for it will change your life. But you desire the Revelation, for it will change your life.

It is your conflict of mind that blinds you. It is the purposes that run counter to one another that keep you in a state of confusion and do not allow you to see.

We are the Ones who have brought all of the Revelations into the world.

For God does not speak. God is not a person or a personage or a personality or a singular awareness. To think like this is to underestimate the Creator and to overestimate yourself.

It is We who spoke to Jesus and the Buddha, the Mohammad and other teachers and seers through the ages who have brought a greater clarity into the world—to the prophets in every age and to the Messengers who only come at great turning points for humanity.

You cannot worship Us. You will not know Our names.

For you must now become responsible and utilize the skills and the power the Creator has given you in service to a world of increasing need, turbulence and upheaval.

Do not prostrate yourself to the Creator if you are unwilling to carry out what you were sent here to do, if you cannot take the Steps to Knowledge, if you have the arrogance to think you can determine your fate and your destiny and fulfillment.

Do not be hypocritical. Do not fall down and worship the God whom you cannot serve or will not serve.

It is better then to live your self-determined life and face all of the hazards of this than it is to worship a God whom you cannot serve.

And if you cannot respond to the Revelation, then what are you doing here now?

Every Messenger has been persecuted. Every Messenger has been misunderstood. Every New Revelation has been resisted and denied and disputed.

There is no time for this now. The fate of humanity will be determined in the next twenty years—the condition of the world, the condition of the human family, the fate and the future of human civilization.

You are no longer alone in the world or even in the universe, of course. You do not know what is occurring and what is coming over the horizon because you are too afraid to see and too arrogant, assuming that you know. That is why the Revelation must be given to show you what you cannot see and do not know beyond human speculation and estimation. This is embedded in all of the Teachings of the New Message.

This is the New Message. Struggle against this and you struggle against your own recognition.

For you must come to know of the greater mind and the greater strength the Creator has given you.

Taught in every religion, but clouded and obscured by every religion, this is what must be recognized now.

God is not managing the world. God is not creating the catastrophes, the storms, the earthquakes, the floods, the droughts.

God is watching to see how humanity will deal with a world it has changed—a new world, a new and unpredictable world.

Humanity is emerging into a Greater Community of life in the universe because others are here to seek influence and domination of a world of great value and importance.

But the people do not see. They do not hear. And if they think at all, it is to create an understanding that affirms their ideas and their beliefs.

So the peoples do not see. The nations do not prepare. And the destructive behavior continues.

We watch over the world. We have been watching for a very long time.

We are those that God has sent to oversee humanity's development and evolution and to receive the Revelations that are then given to the Messengers, to receive the insights that are given to the prophets, to sound the warnings, to provide the blessings and now to provide a preparation for a world unlike the past you have experienced and for a future where humanity will have to contend with the Greater Community itself.

God will not save humanity by driving away the evil, by ending the problems that humanity has created or the problems it must face as a natural part of its evolution.

To think of this is to misunderstand your relationship with the Divine, as you now live in a state of Separation.

But the Separation was never completed because there is a part of you that is still connected to God.

This We call Knowledge. And this will prove to be the decisive factor in the outcome of your personal life—the meaning and the value of your life—and whether humanity can prepare, adapt and create in a new world, in a new set of circumstances.

Never before has such a Revelation been given to the human family, for it was not needed.

You have created a civilization in the world. Fractured and divided it is, but it is a civilization.

You have become increasingly interdependent between your nations and cultures. This was the intention of the Creator, for this is the natural evolution of humanity and all intelligent races in the universe.

Now you must face the next great threshold—a world in decline, a world of declining resources, a world of declining stability, a world of diminishing food and water, a world where a growing humanity will have to face the conditions of the world. For this you need the New Revelation.

The past Revelations of the Creator cannot prepare you for the Great Waves of change. They cannot prepare you for your destiny in the Greater Community. They cannot prepare you for the great thresholds that are now upon you and will be upon you increasingly.

You do not have answers in the face of these things. That is why the Revelation is being given. For humanity now needs to be advised and warned, blessed and given the preparation for a future that will be unlike the past.

Hear these words, not with your intellect but with your heart. They speak to a greater truth within you—a greater truth beyond concepts, beliefs and ideas.

They speak to a natural resonance within you, a natural affinity, a natural inclination, a natural direction that lives within you every moment, beyond the realm and the reach of the intellect.

This is a communication to your deeper nature—to amplify it, to call it forth, to set it in contrast to your ideas, your beliefs and your activities as they exist today.

You are unprepared. God has sent the preparation.

You are unaware. God is providing the awareness.

You are uncertain. God is calling you to the center of certainty within yourself.

You are conflicted. God is providing the pathway out of conflict.

You are self-demeaning and demeaning of others. God is restoring to you your true value and purpose in the world.

The world is changing, but you do not see. God has given you the eyes to see and the ears to hear, but they are different from what you do today and what you understand today.

Humanity will fail without the New Revelation. The world will become ever darker, more dangerous and conflicted without the Revelation.

Humanity will falter and fail in the face of its own errors and lack of clarity.

The resources of the world will be spent through conflict, competition and war. People will rise up against their governments. People will rise up against one another.

There will be untold conflict in the future, greater and more continuous than anything you have seen before.

It is the New Revelation that holds the missing ingredients to your understanding, the key to your awareness and the source of your power, strength and determination.

For this you must have a serious mind, take your life seriously and begin to attend to the greater needs and requirements of your life.

That is why God has sent the Revelation.

This is the Revelation. We are the Revelation.

There are no heroes to worship now, no individuals to deify, only greater responsibility to be assumed and a greater wisdom to be utilized.

There is no escape through personal enlightenment. There is no running away.

There is no self-deception. There is only greater resonance and responsibility, greater sacrifice and contribution.

That is what will save the world. That is what will save humanity's freedom and self-determination in a universe where freedom is rare and must be protected very carefully.

This is what will restore dignity to the individual and the ability to contribute something of greater power and significance, no matter what your circumstances may be.

Hear these words—not with your ideas, your beliefs or your contentions, but with your heart, your deeper nature.

For God can only speak to what God has created in you. God did not create your social personality. God did not create your ideas and beliefs. God did not create your decisions, your failures and your regrets.

God can only speak to what God created in you, which is something deeper, more pervasive and more natural within you.

The New Message is calling to you. Once you become aware of it, then you must face the challenge of recognition and what this will mean for your life.

People reject the Revelation because they do not want to change. They do not want to have to reconsider their beliefs, their ideas and their position in society.

They cannot dispute the New Message, really. They can only avoid it and contend against it to protect their previous investment and idea of themselves.

Who can contend against the Will and the Wisdom of the Creator, except on spurious grounds?

Here you will see the dilemma facing each person. How honest do they really want to be with themselves, what they see and know? How aware do they really want to be of themselves, their situation and the world around them? How responsible are they willing to be to bring their life into balance and to make the difficult decisions they have failed to make before?

Here you will see the intellect parading as a kind of god when, in fact, it is an exquisite servant. That is its purpose and its design.

Here you will see arrogance and ignorance wedded together in a self-deceptive form that so many people adhere to.

You will see what is great and what is small, what is strong and what is weak, what is true and what is false, what is precious and what only pretends to be precious.

The Revelation reveals everything.

It calls on you to follow what is great within you and to manage what is small. It does not speak of any middle ground in this regard.

You cannot have everything. You cannot have your future and your past together because they are not compatible.

It is only through disappointment and failure that you come to see that you are not living the life you were meant to live and that you are not being honest and true to yourself and honest and true with others—a harsh but necessary reckoning in a time of reckoning, a time of realization, a time of Revelation.

Listen to these words—not with your ideas, your assumptions, not with your defenses, not with arrogance, pride or foolishness, but with your deeper nature, for that is what must be revealed to you.

That is part of the Revelation.

CHAPTER 3

THE ENGAGEMENT

As revealed to
Marshall Vian Summers
on April 16, 2011
in Boulder, Colorado

Today We shall speak of God, the Higher Authority.

The Higher Authority is speaking to you now, speaking through the Angelic Presence, speaking to a part of you that is the very center and source of your Being, speaking beyond your social conditioning, beyond your ideas and beliefs and the ideas and beliefs of your culture and even your religion.

The Higher Authority has a Message for the world and for each person in the world. The Message is more than an idea. It is more than even a set of ideas. It is a calling and a confirmation, calling you to respond and confirming that there is a deeper nature within you and within all the people of the world. The confirmation is a turning point in your ability to respond.

The Power and the Presence preside over the physical universe, a universe far greater and more expansive than what you can possibly imagine, and even beyond the physical universe to the greater realms of Creation itself, which is something that few people in the world have even considered to be possible.

And yet the Higher Authority speaks to you in your most private place, the center of your Being, deep beneath the surface of your mind.

This is your greatest relationship and the Source of meaning and purpose in all of your relationships with people, with places and even with things.

You need this Higher Authority now to speak to the deeper part of you, to acquaint you with the deeper part of you and to prepare you for living in a new world and for engaging with a universe of intelligent life, that is the Greater Community of life. You know not of these things, but they are part of you.

Perhaps you have experienced your deeper nature in times of clarity, times of prescience and times even of disappointment, when you were able to hear beyond your desires and your fears and the desires and fears of others.

The Higher Authority is calling to you, calling to you down through the Ancient Corridors of your mind, calling to you beyond your beliefs and your preoccupations.

For God has spoken again and the Word and the Sound are in the world. It is a deeper communication, far deeper and more profound than the intellect can comprehend.

It speaks of a greater purpose and a deeper responsibility and a greater association, both within this world and beyond. And through this association, you become a bridge—a bridge to the world, a bridge to your Ancient Home from which you have come and to which you will return.

People want many things. They have great fears—the fear of losing, the fear of not having, the fear of deprivation, the fear of oppression, the fear of pain and suffering and the pain of death.

But the Higher Authority speaks beyond all of these things. It is the Creator speaking to Creation.

Creation within you is the deeper mind We call Knowledge. It is the permanent part of you. It is the part of you that existed before this life and that will exist after this life, journeying through the realms of Separation, guided only by the power of the Voice.

People want many things. They have great fears. Many people have firm beliefs. But the Higher Authority speaks beyond these things to all who can see and hear and who can respond at a deeper level.

You cannot evaluate this. It is greater than your mind. You cannot debate this, for it is beyond your capabilities.

It is mysterious because it is pervasive. Its origin is beyond this world and all worlds, so you cannot imagine it.

But the experience is so deep that it can alter the course of your life and awaken you from your dream of Separation, calling you out of your preoccupations and your associations and everything so that you may hear the Ancient Voice, so ancient that it speaks of a life beyond your reckoning. But a life that is your life.

God knows what is coming over the horizon. God knows why you are here. God has sent you here for a purpose. Your plans and goals rarely account for this.

It is something greater. It is something more simple and less grandiose. It is something essential to your Being and to your nature and to your design.

It is the most primary relationship you have, the deepest love, the greatest affinity. It unites you with yourself and brings your life into focus.

It calls you out of situations that are harmful or that have no promise for you. It calls you into a greater participation in the world, guided by the mysterious Ancient Voice, a Voice unlike anything you have ever heard, deeper than anything you have ever felt, greater than anything you can see or touch.

People want many things. They are driven by great fear. Even their pleasures are full of fear and apprehension.

But the Ancient Voice is beyond fear, and when you respond, you are beyond fear.

Who can say what this is? Who can evaluate this?

Do not be stupid and think in terms of productivity. Do not be analytical. For this is happening at a deeper and more profound level.

Do not shrink from this. For this is your life, your purpose and your calling.

The Presence and the Grace are with you. But you are looking at other things. Your mind is elsewhere. That which redeems you and restores you is with you now. But you are looking in the other direction.

The Revelation is in the world. God has come again with a greater Message for humanity and a preparation for a difficult and hazardous future for the human family.

What is this? What does it mean? Why is it happening? How do you prepare?

Only the Revelation can answer these questions. Setting yourself apart you cannot answer these questions.

People want many things. They are very distracted. They are very preoccupied. But they do not know where they are or what they are doing. Their goals are the goals of society for the most part. They do not know where they are going in life or why they are here or who sent them and what will restore them and fulfill them and give their life purpose and direction.

The Ancient Voice is speaking to you now. And you will hear the Ancient Voice responding within yourself, for your connection is very deep. It is like the rivers that run underground under the desert, underground rivers of the purest water but which cannot be seen from the surface and which cannot be found except by other means.

While you live your life at the surface, deep within you, you are connected to the Divine. And this connection is experienced through the Calling and the response, by following a deeper Voice and a greater direction.

People ask Why? Why is this happening? They must stop and listen and learn to listen to bring their attention fully into this moment so they can hear and feel and see that the Revelation is stirring within them.

So the Revelation stirs, the Revelation within each person. This is how God speaks to the world at the time of Revelation. This is relationship at the deepest and most significant level.

You cannot break away from God. For God goes everywhere with you. God is with you every moment, in every activity that you do.

Only in your thoughts can you be separate, associating yourself with other things, identifying with other things. But the Ancient Voice is within you, calling you to respond, guiding you, holding you back.

To understand your deeper premonitions and the urgings of your heart, you must begin to listen. Listen within yourself. Listen to the world without judgment and condemnation. Listen for the signs of what is coming. Listen to how you must respond. Listen to who to be with and who not to be with.

Here you do not follow fear. Here there is no condemnation. Here there is a greater discernment and a greater recognition.

God has put Knowledge within you to guide you and to protect you and to lead you to a greater life and participation in the world. It resides beyond the realm and the reach of the intellect. It is happening at a deeper level.

Once you begin to experience this, you begin to gain a greater discernment. You become careful about what you do and who you associate with. You listen deeply to others to see if you should participate with them and what they are communicating to you.

People believe many things, but they know very little. They are living at the surface of the mind, which is turbulent and chaotic and governed by the winds and the passions of the world.

Their beliefs are a substitute for the deeper relationship. Their preoccupations are an avoidance of the greater engagement they are destined to have.

Standing apart, they cannot see. They cannot know. They cannot respond. They are dominated by their thoughts, by their mind, by their reactions. They are slaves, living slavishly.

But the Mystery is within them. It is the most important thing in life. Beyond achieving goals, securing wealth and companionship and recognition in society, it is the most important thing because it is the arena of a greater engagement.

The Mystery is the source of everything important. All the great inventions and contributions, the great relationships, the great experiences—they all come from the Mystery—who you are, why you are here, what is calling you, your greater association, your destiny with certain people in the world, your ability to find your way while everyone around you is sleeping, dreaming and unresponsive. This is a journey you must take or your life will be a troubled dream and no more.

When you return to your Spiritual Family after you leave this world, they will look at you to see if you have accomplished your task, if you made the deeper connection. And you will know if you have or you have not.

There is no judgment and condemnation, only recognition here. Here what was mysterious before becomes reality itself and your priorities are clear. There are no distractions. There is no resistance.

And you will want to return, saying to yourself, "This time I will remember. I know now. I can see now. I will remember."

But you must remember while you are here. That makes all the difference. That is the beginning of everything important. That is the turning point of your life.

It is only mysterious because you have been divorced from it, caught up in the world of form, lost in the world, growing up as an individual, adapting to a difficult and changing world. Then something comes to remind you, and you begin to feel that the Mystery is with you and in you and influencing you.

Its Source is beyond the physical reality, for who you are is beyond the physical reality. Where you are going ultimately is beyond the physical reality. But you are meant to be here because you have been sent here for a purpose. That is the Mystery.

We speak of these things to engage you at a deeper level, to call forth that which is authentic, to speak to a part of you you barely know which is the greater part of you. And this part of you will respond because of Our ancient commitment together.

You are afraid of this, but you desire it at the same time. It is a natural desire, more natural than anything else you are doing or could do in the world.

It is the Engagement.

CHAPTER 4

GOD HAS SPOKEN AGAIN

As revealed to
Marshall Vian Summers
on February 24, 2011
in Boulder, Colorado

God has spoken again.

God has spoken again because the world is facing its greatest travails, its most difficult challenges.

The human family has created an environmental calamity that has the power to undermine its civilization—a calamity of many factors; a calamity that will alter your environment, that will deplete your soils, that will dry up your rivers; a calamity that will bring an end to your growth and expansion; a calamity that has been the product of decades and centuries of misuse of the world, with no thought of tomorrow, as if the world were an endless bounty that could be exploited without limit.

And the religions of the world, which were all initiated by God, are in contention with each other—sometimes violently, often vehemently— in contention with each other, vying for precedence and recognition, claiming in many cases to be the greatest or even the only true manifestation of God's Revelation, the one true path which must be followed.

God has spoken again because humanity has plundered the world and is now facing a predicament that could lead to great deprivation and conflict.

God has spoken again because religion has failed to find its unity, except amongst a very few individuals and organizations.

It has failed to bridge the tribal identities of people that had to be overcome sufficiently for a world community to be established—to transcend one's immediate group, one's regional identity, one's unique customs and culture, to become part of a world community.

This is evolution for humanity, an evolution that leads to great diversity of cultural expression, but enables people to live and to communicate and to share their creations with one another.

God has spoken again even though there are many who say that this is not possible, that the last prophet [had] the great and final message to the world. But what person can say this? Even God's Messengers cannot make such claims.

For God communicates when God wills and is not bound by human ideas or beliefs. What arrogance to think that the Creator of all the universes is going to be impeded by human presumption and human admonition.

That is why again God has spoken, for there is great correction that must come to your understanding of the Divine Presence and Power in your life and in the world and beyond the world within a Greater Community of life in the universe.

Humanity stands at the threshold of space, the threshold of encountering a Greater Community of life—a Greater Community that is far more complex, demanding and challenging than anything the human family has ever encountered.

It is as if humanity were an adolescent entering an adult world, full of presumption and self-importance, of course, but unaware and dangerously naïve of the realities and difficulties of that adult world.

The religions of the world, which were given to build human civilization, were not designed to prepare humanity for the Greater Community. That was not their purpose or function, you see.

But now the evolutionary progress and process have brought humanity to this great threshold. Living in a world of declining resources and growing population, it must now face the reality, the difficulty and the great opportunity of facing a Greater Community of life.

For beyond your fears, beyond your anxieties, beyond your avoidance and denial, you will be able to see that the Great Waves of change that are coming to the world and humanity's encounter with a universe of intelligent life are the two greatest things, the two greatest motivations that will lead humanity to finally cooperate and to establish a functioning and equitable world order, a world stability that has never been found before.

This stability cannot be under oppressive rule, or it will not succeed. It is now being generated out of necessity. For nations competing and fighting against one another will only deplete the world even further and faster. And with a changing climate and a changing environment, nations will have to cooperate if they are to survive and to provide for their peoples.

It is life at such a simple, elemental level, lost to the modern mind that thinks of its desires and its fears, its fantasies and its creations with such obsessive indulgence that it cannot see the realities of life itself.

Despoil your environment and it will undermine you. It will work against you. Fight with each other, and war will become perpetual. The [old] grievances will be renewed, and new grievances [will be] established.

The world needs a New Revelation. For Christianity cannot save the world. Islam cannot save the world. Buddhism and Hinduism cannot save the world. And Judaism was never designed to save the world.

Now that there is a world community of great interdependence and great fragility and great vulnerability, both to internal collapse and to external competition and intervention, it is time for humanity to grow up. It is time for a change of heart, for people of all nations—a reckoning of the reality of the situation, a comprehension of the Great Waves of change and their power to affect and undermine a stable world.

It is time for God to speak again. God knows this, of course, though few people recognize it.

Many people are waiting for the fulfillment of their early prophecies—the return of the Imam, the Maitreya [or] the Jesus. But they will not return, you see. And those coming to claim these titles and these identities will not be the spiritually enlightened or the spiritually endowed, but those from the Greater Community who are here to take advantage of human foolishness and expectation.

God has spoken again. If you could honestly recognize the need for this—the need for this in your life, in your community, in your family, in your nation, between your nations—then you could see that a New Revelation is required and that you are actually living at a time of Revelation.

But here you must be very clear, for God is not giving you a new superhero to believe in. God is not giving you a massive doctrine to adhere to under the grave threat of punishment if you should fail. God is not asking you to believe in one teacher. God is not asking you to have one theology or one philosophy.

God is bringing, instead, the power of Knowledge to the individual and with that power, responsibility in service to the world. God is not going to give humanity a new idea which it will fight over in dissent. It is going to give you something more fundamental, something you could really only give to a world community that is facing great peril and upheaval.

This is a more advanced Revelation—not given now in simple stories or anecdotes, not given in admonitions, not pictured in simple pastoral images, not given in mystical identities with the promise of enlightenment, but given to bring the individual to a state of recognition and a sense of responsibility, not only to oneself, but to rescuing human civilization itself.

People will not understand this at first because they do not see the great peril facing humanity. They think that life will be as it has been before, perhaps more problematic, more difficult, more uncertain. They do not realize they are living in a new world—a world that has changed imperceptibly, a world that will not be the same as the world that they grew up in, the world of their parents or ancestors. And they will see that without the guidance of Knowledge within themselves, they are lost in this world—this world that will become ever more disturbing, ever more uncertain.

At a certain point, you cannot run from this. You cannot live in a state of fantasy or denial, projecting your blame and hostility on your parents or your culture or organizations or governments.

There has to be a reckoning, you see, and the sooner this reckoning happens for the individual, the sooner they begin to take stock of their life.

But what will guide humanity is what influences and determines your decisions. Whether you are the leader of a nation or a poor person living on the outside of the city, it is what informs your decisions and what you can hear and see within yourself and others that will make all the difference in what you choose to do in the face of the Great Waves of change and the degree of wisdom you can bring to your own circumstances, no matter how difficult they are.

God is giving to humanity something humanity does not even know it needs—the one key element, the missing piece, the part that only God can provide, the strength, the power and vision that only God can provide.

Without this, your technology will not save you. Your ingenuity will not save you. Luck will not save you. Denial or avoidance will not save you. Immersing yourself in hobbies and distractions will not save you. That is why God has spoken again.

The Message is honest. It is so honest that people will run away from it. It is so honest that it will confuse the person receiving it at first, perhaps. It is so honest because it asks you to be so honest.

It asks you to be what God created in you and to manage that part of yourself that is a product of living in the world—a big demand, but a fair demand if you are going to be able to face a declining world and to face the realities of the Greater Community, where childishness and foolishness will hurt you and make you weak.

The world has changed. God's great Revelations must now be given the next stage of their expression—not to replace them but to uplift them and to cleanse them and to bring them into harmony with one another. They are all pathways to Knowledge, you see. That is what they really are.

They have been turned into other things by governments, by individuals and institutions, by nations seeking power and dominance. They have been alloyed with culture and customs and local perceptions to a point where their essential emphasis and purpose can be difficult to discern.

This is to bring people back to the essence of spirituality, which is the power and the presence of Knowledge in the individual, the power and the presence of Knowledge—this greater intelligence that God has given to each person, working through groups and nations of people, supporting freedom and forgiveness, recognition, communication, work, effort, responsibility.

This is not simply an option now, for the world you are facing will be much more difficult and much more demanding. And the decisions you will have to make will be very consequential for you and for others.

You cannot be fooling around in the face of the Great Waves of change. You are standing at the threshold of the Greater Community. Only God can prepare you for these two great realities. And God is giving you the essential components of that preparation.

God gives the world what it needs, but the people cannot see it. They want a warrior leader. They want a military power. They want a Barabbas, not a Jesus. They want the lord of the lands, not the Lord of the Heavens. They want material power. They want material resolution. They want their problems fixed for them. They want to give over the reins instead of receive the gift of responsibility.

The miracle of the New Message is the miracle of all the Revelations. It is the miracle of personal revelation. It is the miracle of personal redemption. It is the miracle of personal and individual responsibility and contribution to society and to others. It is the miracle of giving. It is the miracle of forgiveness. It is the miracle of resonating with another at a deeper level, beyond the realm and the reach of the intellect. It is the miracle of your true reality expressing itself in a difficult and temporary world.

What will inform your decisions will make all the difference in determining the outcome. God has given you the voice and the conscience to guide you, but it is not your voice or your conscience. It is part of a greater Voice and a greater conscience.

God is not ruling the world, governing the weather. God is not the source of calamities and catastrophes, hurricanes and earthquakes and floods. That is just nature functioning.

God has sent you into this difficult and unpredictable world, as beautiful as it is, to reclaim the power of Knowledge and with this power be guided to give what you are designed to give specifically where your contribution can have the greatest impact.

This all transcends the human intellect, of course, for you will never understand the workings of Creation and Heaven, which extend far beyond the physical universe, which itself is so vast that no race has ever been able to comprehend its entirety or its full meaning.

Here the practical and the mystical unite. Here the inner and the outer make their essential connection. Here the mind is governed by a greater intelligence so the intellect's tremendous capabilities can be wisely used and applied. Here people take responsibility not only for bringing their affairs into order and balance, but also to see what they must do to assist the human family wherever their gifts can be given.

You will have to look on the world very compassionately in the future. You will see much failure and loss. You will see great foolishness and even the recurrent indulgences of humanity become ever more extreme.

You will have to forgive and look upon the world with compassion. You cannot be fully detached from it, for you are connected to it, you are sent to serve it and your purpose and destiny are related to it.

The goal is not [inner] peace. The goal is contribution. Even the greatest saints have had to recognize this and be sent out into the world to teach and preach and contribute wherever they can.

Your achievements in the world, or even your spiritual achievements, are all to be used to serve, to lighten the burden of those around you, to encourage people to return to the Power and the Presence that is their Source and their connection to the Divine—using whatever beliefs or symbols or images or personages they find most inspiring.

What is essential and important is the pursuit and the recognition that you live with two minds—the worldly mind and the deeper mind of Knowledge.

This is for everyone, not just for one tribe, one group or one time in history or to meet one great episode in the long story of humanity's presence in this world.

God has spoken again now of greater things—things beyond the ordinary and things that are extremely ordinary and important. God has spoken of the Greater Community, the Great Waves of change, the meaning of your inner reality [and] the essential pursuit to reclaim your connection to Knowledge, which is here to guide you, protect you and lead you to your greater accomplishments in life.

It is a tremendous breakthrough for the individual. And it will be individuals that will make all the difference in deciding the fate and the future of humanity.

And what informs their decisions—whether it be ambition, belief, fear, pride and their previous understanding or the greater inspiration that only Knowledge can provide—will determine the outcome in every situation.

God has spoken again. You must come to the Revelation to see. Do not be foolish and stand apart and try to judge it or understand it, for you will not understand it. And to judge it merely is to demonstrate your foolishness and your lack of honesty.

This is a great time of Revelation. It is a great time of preparation for the future. It is a great time to bring your life into balance and harmony and to prepare yourself for living in a new world, a demanding world, but also a redeeming world if humanity chooses to follow what God has provided.

CHAPTER 5

THE SEAL OF THE PROPHETS

As revealed to
Marshall Vian Summers
on May 21, 2014
in Boulder, Colorado

It is very important now that We speak of the Seal of the Prophets so that the people of the world may understand what this really means and why it is important to protect God's great Revelations, which are only given at certain key turning points in humanity's development and evolution.

The great Revelations are so very important for the world. They provide the building blocks of human civilization.

Now God has spoken again to protect human civilization from internal disintegration and collapse and from subjugation from forces in the universe who seek to take advantage of human conflict and ignorance.

It is a threshold that was long anticipated and was destined to arrive, and it would arrive at a time when humanity had begun to establish a world civilization—certainly not a perfect civilization, but a civilization nonetheless.

It would happen when certain conditions were met and when humanity's vulnerability to its own errors would grow to such a point that human civilization itself would be endangered through environmental decline and disruption and through the Earth becoming plundered to a point where it could no longer provide sufficiently for a growing humanity.

It would wait to a point when humanity's vulnerability to the universe would reach a critical threshold. For the Earth has been long observed by certain races for their own purposes and designs.

God knows this, of course, for this is part of any world's evolution— any world that has been a fountainhead of a race's emergence or any world that has been cultivated by visitors from beyond. It is predictable. It will happen sooner or later. And the time for this now for humanity has come.

God protects the great Revelations with a Seal. The Seal means that the Angelic Assembly will not provide another great Revelation until the Lord of the universe indicates that it must be so. It is their Seal, to protect the Revelations from usurpation, from plagiarism and from those who proclaim themselves to be emissaries and messengers, which inevitably happens following a great Revelation for the world.

People of the Earth will not know this Seal exists. It is not something they can touch. It is not written in their constitutions. It is not widely understood or accepted.

But amongst the Angelic Presence and Assembly who oversees this world, it is a very clear mandate and must be established, or the great Revelations can be polluted beyond recognition. They will be affected and altered by humankind over time, through ignorance and corruption and through the misuse of adoption. But the Seal in Heaven is complete, you see.

However, at a certain point, God will break the Seal, for a New Revelation must come. For the great Teachings that were given before would be insufficient to meet the real needs of the human family as a whole.

The interval between the great Revelations will be very long, in most cases, for they are sufficient to meet humanity's needs for a great period of time to come.

But now you have reached the great threshold where God has spoken again—a great threshold for which humanity is ignorant and unprepared, a great threshold that the great Revelations given in the ancient times cannot address. They were not designed for this. They were not given for this purpose. They were critical in building human civilization, a world civilization over time.

But now human civilization as it stands today is threatened both from within and from without, so severely threatened that God has spoken again, for the risks are too high, the dangers are too great, human ignorance is too profound.

Even the great Revelations given before are fractured and contentious within themselves and between one another. They cannot prepare humanity for a Greater Community of life in the universe. They cannot prepare humanity for a world in environmental decline—the greatest change that could happen to any civilization in any world. They were not designed for this purpose.

God knows this, of course. But humanity does not know. It does not realize what is coming over the horizon. It does not understand its condition in light of life around it in the universe. It does not know the state of the Earth sufficiently to see how much it has overtaken and overspent its natural inheritance in this world. It is on a reckless course of self-destruction and disintegration over time.

The great changes that will come to the planet itself are sufficient to reduce human civilization severely, if humanity is not prepared.

Here the Seal is broken, for a New Revelation must be given. The Seal was broken after the life of Jesus when Muhammad was given his great mission on Earth. And now the Seal is being broken again in God's New Revelation [for] the world.

Here you must understand that the great Messengers have all come from the Angelic Assembly, sent into the world for a great mission, sent into the world at great turning points and opportunities. They have all come from the Assembly. They all have a common Source. They are not sons of God. They are not the center of the universe.

They have come from the Assembly that oversees this world, a world of great importance and significance in the universe because humanity has kept its spiritual awareness alive. Despite its many errors and tragic history—great conflicts and great misfortunes it has wrought upon itself and upon the world—it is still a world of great promise and significance.

God will create a new Seal when the Proclamation at this time is complete, and it will last for centuries.

People will still claim to have messages from God or to be prophets or redeemers. But the Angelic Assembly will not give them what it would be required to give them for this to be really true and authentic. In this way, Heaven does what it can to protect the great Revelations, which are so vulnerable to human misuse and misunderstanding.

God's New Revelation for the world at this great turning point is the most expansive ever given to the world—given to a literate world now, a world of global commerce and communication, a world of global dangers and risks, given now with its own commentary to limit the possibility of it being misconstrued and misapplied in the future, given with great repetition, said in many ways to give the greatest opportunity for people to truly understand what they are receiving and why it must be given at this time.

God's New Revelation for the world contains a warning, a blessing and a great preparation. Without the preparation, you could not respond to the warning. Without the warning, you would not understand the importance of the preparation. And without the blessing, you would not have the strength or know where to turn within yourself or between one another for the courage and determination to do what must be done for the world, to understand the real meaning of your purpose here and why you have come at this great turning point.

This is not a gift for the elect few, or a few chosen individuals, or for the richest and the most privileged amongst you. It is given to the whole world, given in the simplest terms, given in the clearest possible way, given with great strength, speaking to almost every avenue of human experience, given to give humanity this one great chance to restore the world and to prepare itself for the Greater Community of life, for which it must now learn to respond.

Think not this is irrelevant to your needs, for this is the world you have come to serve. These two great events will determine in all matters, in all manner of ways, what kind of life you will be able to have, what will limit your life and what can draw forth from you your greater strengths and the greater purpose that lies hidden within you beneath the surface of your mind. Think not this does not speak to you, for you have been sent into the world for this.

What happens in this world and beyond this world, regarding this world, will determine the fate and the future of every person alive today and of their children and the generations to come. That is how powerful this is. That is how necessary this is.

It [the New Message from God] will change your understanding of religion and bring great clarity here. It will establish the unity of all religions and how they have built upon one another to provide the true moral and ethical foundation for human conduct and understanding.

But you are living in a different world now, and you are facing a very different world in the future—a world of diminishing resources and unstable climate, a world that will affect everybody's life, rich or poor, in all corners of the world.

So great is the need. So great is the risk. So great is the influence and the power of this that God has spoken again and sent a new Messenger into the world. Sent from the Angelic Assembly he is, akin to all those who were sent before. They stand with him, for he is the Messenger of this time, of this era and of the times to come for a very long time.

The Seal will be with him, and Heaven will watch to see who can respond to his presence on Earth. For he is an older man now and does not have a long time to teach this.

[He] has spent his life receiving a Revelation more vast and more complete than anything that has ever been given to humanity before.

It will reveal the meaning of life in the universe. It will reveal what is coming over the horizon of your life and of the whole world. It will reveal the true nature of human spirituality at a higher level, at a level called Knowledge. It will reveal what humanity must learn to create real cooperation here on Earth and to end its ceaseless conflicts and its terrible plundering of the world. For this is the only world you will have that can sustain you.

The universe around you will not be yours to conquer or to explore beyond this solar system. There are great dangers there, of which humanity knows nothing at all. It is still looking through primitive eyes, the eyes of ignorance and hopeful expectation. It does not know what it is dealing with in a Greater Community of life in the universe.

God must now provide this, at least sufficiently, so humanity can prepare and act with wisdom and concern for the future, rather than merely acting out of expediency for the moment.

This has everything to do with who you are—your deeper nature, why you are the way you are and why you are designed the way you are—which is something you cannot understand until you realize it is for a greater purpose, which you have yet to really discover.

You must accept that the Seal of the Prophets has been broken. Not by a person, not by a religion, but by God, who communicates to the world through the Angelic Presence and Assembly that oversees this world and the progress and evolution of the human family.

Here there will be great clarity about the questions of religion, the meaning of your life, the destiny of humanity and the great challenges to come, for which humanity must prepare at this time.

Do not shrink from this. Do not fall into the shadows of your own preoccupations. Do not despair. For God has given you a deeper strength within yourself to enable you to respond, to prepare to face a larger world and to experience a greater life.

You do not understand what this means yet, but in time it will become as clear as day. For God has given you the eyes to see and the ears to hear, but they are not the eyes that you see with now or the ears that you hear with now. Yet they are within you—deeper within you.

This is the true strength of your life. This is the true strength of the human family. It is this that will make all the difference in the outcome for your life on Earth here and for the future and destiny of humanity.

Only God's New Revelation for the world can reveal these things to you now. Without this, humanity will continue in its desperate combative fall, its desperate combative trajectory in life, depleting the world so critically that it will not be able to sustain human civilization in any kind of recognizable form. You will fall prey to dominating forces of the universe, and everything that you have created of value will be lost.

It is only God's Revelation for the world that can reveal this to you clearly, without distortion, without the interests of any foreign race being involved, without any manipulation or deception whatsoever.

In your heart, you will respond because at a deeper level you are still connected to God. Whether you are religious or not, whether you have a faith tradition or not, you are still connected. And that is the promise of your future redemption, the source of your greater strength and your greater resolution of whatever has happened to you before.

The Seal of the Prophets has been broken again by God. It was destined to be broken once humanity reached a certain destination, reached a great turning point where it would be facing challenges never seen by the human family as a whole before, facing a world in decline and the realities of the universe around you.

God has given the clarity now to understand what all the great traditions were really talking about, before they were changed and adopted and utilized through generations by individuals and governments for their own purposes.

Here you honor all the great Messengers and understand their mission on Earth more completely, in a clear light. For there should be no contention and competition between the religions of the world, for they were all initiated by God, and they have all been changed by man.

The Seal has been broken, but it will be re-established once God's New Revelation is complete, and once the Messenger has time to present it in his own time, which must occur now for the Revelation to be truly, completely authentic. It cannot be assembled later by those who did not know him.

It has been his great task to receive the largest Revelation ever given to this world—to compile it, to assure its accuracy, to learn of it so it could be taught, to understand it completely while he is a person here in the world, to assemble around him courageous individuals who would assist him in these great tasks so that within his life, the Revelation could be rendered in its pure form, solving a dilemma that has plagued the earlier Revelations for humanity.

The Blessing is upon you. It is upon the world, but it comes with great urgency and necessity. It is not a thing that you use to try to enrich yourself or to dabble with. You must approach it with reverence and great seriousness and the willingness to see what it really means for you and for the world.

It must speak to people of all faith traditions and all nations and cultures.

It must be free of any kind of ownership by an existing religious institution beyond what the Messenger has established to receive, to prepare and to render it into the world.

He will need your support. But you must learn of this and apply it to your life to understand. You cannot stand apart from it and understand it, for that is not possible with a great Revelation born of Heaven for the well-being and protection of the world.

May the Blessing be upon the Messenger and all those who assist him in his remaining years on Earth. And may those who have courage, humility and the great need to understand, receive this in time to recognize its essential importance for their lives and for the future of this world.

CHAPTER 6

THE MISSION OF THE MESSENGER

As revealed to
Marshall Vian Summers
on April 10, 2012
in Boulder, Colorado

God has sent a New Revelation into the world, unlike anything that has been sent for over a thousand years.

A Messenger has been sent into the world—a Messenger who led a somewhat ordinary life, a Messenger who is a humble man and who has been in a very long preparation for this role.

While others may claim such a title to be a Messenger of God, in truth, there is only one who is sent to the world. Heaven knows this, of course, though people will make other claims and assertions.

People are afraid of the Messenger. They are afraid of what it might mean for them, how it might change their ideas or how it might call them into some kind of greater service or association.

Many people will reject God's New Revelation purely on this basis alone because they are afraid that there is a New Revelation in the world that could alter the course of human history and destiny and that would challenge many of the prevailing notions and beliefs that have become institutionalized and so well established.

But the Creator of all life is not bound by these things and only provides the essential Message and Revelation for the welfare of humanity and for humanity's future and destiny, both within this world and within a Greater Community of life in the universe.

God's New Revelation is more expansive and inclusive and detailed than anything that has ever been brought to the world before. It is being given at a time when the human family has become literate and is participating in a world civilization and economy with international communication. It is a very different environment than any of the previous Revelations, which were very regional in nature and which only spread over a great span of time and through much discord, conflict and violence.

Humanity stands at the threshold of a universe full of intelligent life—a non-human universe that it must now learn to contend with.

And humanity is living in a world of declining resources and environmental instability, unlike anything that has been seen for thousands of years. Even your history cannot account for what this might mean, except the history of the Earth itself.

The Revelation brings its own commentary. It is not simply a mysterious teaching that is left up to human interpretation, as has been the case before.

This Revelation is complete and comprehensive, touching on nearly every aspect of an individual's life and the life of humanity, both now and in the future.

And yet like all the Revelations in history, it speaks of greater things than humanity's concerns today. It speaks of things which will make all the difference in whether humanity chooses to unite in a declining world or whether it will fight and struggle over who has access to the remaining resources.

It will make all the difference in whether humanity can prepare for its engagement with the Greater Community, which is already taking place due to an Intervention in the world today by races who are here to take advantage of human weakness, conflict and expectation.

A Message so great has required a tremendous preparation for the Messenger and for those few individuals who have been called to assist him in his preparation and proclamation.

He is not here to answer every question or to have a solution for every need. His Message speaks to the need of the soul within the individual—the need to reconnect with the Source of life and to gain the strength that God has given every person through the presence of a deeper intelligence within them called Knowledge.

The Messenger is not here to argue or to debate or to take issue with world affairs or the ambitions of different groups, nations or tribes. He is here to bring a Message of Revelation and redemption to the peoples of the whole world, regardless of their individual cultural position or religious affiliation, if they have one at all.

This transcends nations and culture and religious ideology. This transcends the controversies regarding these things because it is a New Message from God for the redemption and preparation of the whole world for a reality and a future that will be very different from the past.

Only God can provide such a thing. For even at this moment, the religions are divided, even within themselves. They are contentious and unable to address adequately the great rising global problems that will overtake humanity in the future if it is unprepared.

Arguing over who has the best religion or the most astounding founder can only harm humanity now. It is divisive and exclusive. It adds to the dilemma and the fracturing of the human family.

God knows better. And the one chosen to bring the Revelation is the perfect one. He has passed the tests. He has not failed the long preparation and all that it required of him and of his family.

People will resist this and resent it and accuse the Messenger of all manner of things. But he is the one. Failure to see his value and his role is a failure on the part of the perceiver, a failure to recognize and to receive the great Blessing that God is now sending into the world.

The Messenger has no pride. He is a humble man, but he must accept the great calling and the greater responsibilities this places upon him and the great travail he will have to face in bringing a New Revelation into the world.

God has spoken again. And God's Revelation is not for some elite group or the culturally privileged, the wealthy and the indulgent. It is for the person at every rank and station of society—of every society, even the most primitive, the most advanced, the most isolated or the most global.

Only the wisdom of the Creator can speak like this, through the Angelic Presence, through the Voice of Revelation, which you are hearing at this moment.

The mission of the Messenger is to bring the Revelation into the world, to find its first respondents, to give them the opportunity to engage with the Revelation and to come to terms with their own deeper nature and calling in life.

That is why a great deal of the Teaching has been given, to pave the way for personal revelation for those who can receive it, adapt to it and apply it in their lives successfully.

Its demands are not great except that it calls for a greater honesty than most people demonstrate at this moment, an honesty not simply to project one's ideas and beliefs upon the world, but to recognize the deeper current of one's life and, in a state of humility and determination, choose to follow that. For that is the power and presence of Knowledge in the individual, which God's Revelation reveals fully for the first time.

Here there are no heroes to worship. Here there is no Judgment Day. Here there is no final test, which nearly everyone would fail anyway.

For God knows better than this. God knows that without Knowledge, people will falter and fail, make foolish mistakes and give their lives over and succumb to dangerous and oppressive forces. For without the Power of God in the individual to guide them, what else would they do but demonstrate their weakness and their confusion and the fact that their life is dominated by others?

You see, the God of your world is the God of the entire Greater Community, the entire universe—a billion, billion, billion races and more, in one galaxy and amongst many galaxies and other dimensions, and the unchanging Creation beyond that. You are dealing with a God now of such greatness and expansion that your ideas and your beliefs pale and falter in the face of such magnificence.

This is the God that has placed Knowledge within you to guide you and bless you and prepare you for a greater life, to take you out of your groveling and your pathetic engagements and self-pity, to restore honor and dignity to you, self-respect, graciousness, compassion and humility.

It is the mission of the Messenger to teach these things, to offer these things, to endure the resistance and the rejection of those who cannot see and will not know.

This is the greater calling, you see. This is what restores the individual and gives the promise for a greater life. This is what brings honor and dignity to all people, even the poorest of the poor, who live in degradation.

This is to establish a greater ethic of unity and cooperation in the face of a world of diminishing resources. Can you even imagine such a world, you who have lived in a state of plenty, perhaps? Can you imagine what this could do to the human family? It could destroy human civilization.

Humanity's encounter with aggressive forces acting surreptitiously in the world could bring down and destroy human civilization.

People do not know this. They do not think of this. Perhaps it is too much for them, they who have given all of their thoughts to little things, afraid of losing their privileges. They do not see the bigger picture, which will determine the outcome for everyone.

But for those who can see and hear, the Revelation will speak to them, and they will be the first to respond. And through them, the Revelation will speak to those who have been more preoccupied and less able to see the great events coming over the horizon. One man cannot do all this. It will take the engagement of many working in concert with the Messenger.

And then you have the problem of people who are self-seeking and aggressive, who believe they are so very important in the universe, claiming to have their own version, acting out of concert with the Messenger, trying to wed the New Revelation with other teachings or with their own ideas.

This is the corruption that happens whenever anything that is pure is brought into the world. And that is why the Revelation is being given before the Proclamation. That is why it is in writing. That is why you can hear the Voice of Revelation for the first time in human history. Such a Voice that spoke to the Jesus, the Buddha and the Muhammad, you can hear.

Can you hear? You who listen to so many other things of little value, can you hear these words? Even if you are doubtful and suspicious, can you hear the Messenger and the Revelation? It is as plain as day, without deception, without complexity, without human commentary to cloud the stream and to pollute the atmosphere of Revelation.

The mission of the Messenger is to establish God's Revelation here sufficiently within his remaining years so that humanity can begin to prepare for a changing world and prepare for its engagement with the Greater Community itself.

This will change your theology. This will change your understanding of God and how God works in the world. This will challenge your fundamental religious beliefs about what redemption means because when you think of God in the Greater Community, it changes everything.

What is Heaven for a billion, billion, billion races and more? What is Hell when you know that God has put Knowledge within you and you can never escape it—its blessing and its redemption?

What is one's religious affiliation with the understanding that there are billions and billions of religions in the universe, either more or less connected to the reality of God's Presence and Power?

Who can say when God will speak again? Who, without arrogance and ignorance, can say that God cannot speak again? Even God's Messengers cannot say that. Even the Angelic Host cannot say that. So what person can claim such authority to determine what God will do next? It is the epitome of arrogance and foolishness.

The mission of the Messenger will have to face all of these things. It will have to face intellectual arrogance. It will have to face outright blind rejection. It will have to face every form of accusation.

This is towards one who is bringing the greatest expression of God's love that has been received in 1400 years. This is directed at one whose life, though facing difficulty and imperfect, is nonetheless a demonstration of the Revelation itself.

For the first time in human history, the whole world can witness the process of Revelation instead of only hearing about it through distant tales and fantastic stories.

For the first time, the human family can hear the Voice of Revelation, read the words of Revelation, not as they were portrayed centuries later by people who did not know the Messenger, not carried on through oral tradition for the benefit of illiterate populations, but something right in this moment.

For humanity does not have centuries to come to terms with this. The change that is underway is too rapid. The convergence of greater forces is too powerful and overwhelming.

Around the world, people are feeling anticipation and anxiety about the direction of the world. Whatever they ascribe these fears to or however they might try to define it, it is because they are feeling the Great Waves of change that are coming to the world. They are feeling that humanity is becoming ever more weak, vulnerable, subject now to forces beyond its awareness.

It is because of this that God has sent the Revelation into the world. It is because of this that the Messenger is here.

Honor him. Respect him. He is not a god, but none of the Messengers were gods. He is not perfect, but none of the Messengers were perfect. He has struggled with the Revelation because all of the Messengers have struggled with their Revelations.

He will be attacked and condemned because all of the Messengers have been attacked and condemned by the very same thoughtlessness, arrogance and ignorance that the Messenger today will have to face, and is facing even at this moment.

His mission is not to build bridges or change governments or rectify every problem and error and injustice in the world.

His mission is to give the secret restoration to the individual and to prepare humanity for the greatest events in human history, which are now upon you and which are coming over the horizon even at this moment.

Humanity will have nothing if it cannot survive in a declining world. Your great works, treasures and art will all be gone.

Humanity will have nothing in the Greater Community, where freedom is so very rare, if it cannot establish wisdom and safeguard its borders and unite its people at least sufficiently enough that they can respond for their mutual welfare, protection and advancement.

In the Light of the Revelation, human folly, ignorance and arrogance are so fully revealed. It is as if a great Light is [shining] upon the world and everything that is dark and secretive, everything that is deceitful and malicious, become exposed in the Light of Revelation—the weakness of people's positions; the pathetic quality of their lives; their great need for restoration, dignity and redemption; human corruption; human deception; those who claim to be religious, who are not religious, but who use religion for power and dominance.

All this will be revealed in the Light of Revelation, and that is why those who will deny the Revelation will have to speak out against it, for it will threaten their position; it will expose their weakness, their errors and their dangerous tendencies.

The Revelation is the product of great Love, for God is not angry with humanity. For God knows that without the power and presence of Knowledge to guide people sufficiently in their own awareness that people will act foolishly, selfishly and destructively.

God knows this. Humanity does not. To understand this is not merely a matter of belief. It is a matter of a deeper recognition, a deeper resonance within oneself, a deeper honesty that you yourself cannot fulfill yourself and that a greater Revelation is greatly needed in the world.

Can people be this honest? Can people be this sober about themselves without condemnation? Can people really take stock of where they are and—whether they are rich or poor, advantaged or disadvantaged— the degree to which their lives have become empty? Can they face this and realize that this emptiness is a calling to God and that God has responded?

The mission of the Messenger is to bring the Revelation to as many people as possible, within his remaining time here on Earth, and for others who will carry on his great work with his blessing, who will carry the New Message into the future, to bring it to ever more people—to the disadvantaged, to the wealthy, to the rich nations, to the poor nations, to the natives living out in nature, to the people of the big cities.

The Revelation is here. It can be studied alone. It can be studied together with others effectively. It can be heard. It can be read. It can be translated clearly. It must be shared. That is the duty of every person who receives it, and it will be your natural desire to do so.

But like all the great Revelations at their time, it will be resisted and be difficult at first, for the world does not know it needs a Revelation from God. The world is not prepared for this, and many people are set against it for different and various reasons.

In time, if you can see this clearly, you will see that the Messenger is demonstrating in a very large sense the true reality of your life—that you were sent into the world to do something important. Perhaps it is not going to be at a grand and global scale. That does not matter.

Everyone was sent into the world for a greater purpose. And the fact that people are not aware of this or cannot find it because of political or religious oppression, [or] that people are blind to it, cannot hear it, cannot feel it, cannot support it in one another—that is the tragedy of the human family. That is the cause for corruption, dissension, conflict, hatred and all of the things that plague the human family and keep it from becoming a greater people in the universe.

All these things that plague humanity stand in the way of its freedom in the Greater Community. All these things now must be realized by enough people—perhaps not everyone, but enough people—so that a greater movement can happen in the world, a greater conscience can be revealed that actually lives within each person at this moment.

To learn of the Revelation means to come back into relationship with Knowledge, which is the part of you that has never left God, that is still in communication, that is wise and uncorrupted by the world, that is unafraid of the world, a wisdom and a strength that is the source of whatever courage and integrity you might have established thus far in your life.

This is the gift of the Messenger. This was the gift of the past Messengers. But their story has been changed. And often their words have been misread.

For all of God's Revelations [are] to restore to the individual the power and the presence of Knowledge, for this is their true conscience, and this is what will bring them to God, in a pure and efficacious way.

The world is blessed because God has spoken again. The world is blessed because the Messenger is in the world.

Receive this blessing. Share it with others. The Revelation is very great. You cannot understand it in a moment. You cannot read it in a sentence. You must come to it seeking its wisdom and relevance for your life and for the world you see.

It is the test, you see. It is the difficulty and the great opportunity of living at the time of Revelation. It is the test—the test for the recipient.

God will not punish those who fail, but they will not be in a position to receive the Revelation and the great empowerment, clarity and blessing it will bring into their lives and affairs.

God does not punish the wicked, for God knows that without Knowledge, wickedness will arise.

That is why the Revelation calls people to the greater intelligence that lives within them that is fundamental to all good things that can happen for them and for the world.

This brings great clarification to your understanding of the Divine Presence and Power, how God works in the world—the God of the universes.

This is your great opportunity, the greatest moment in human history, the great turning point for the human family that will determine whether it will be a free and coherent civilization in the future or whether it will decay and fall under foreign persuasion.

It is the great turning point, the great challenge, the great opportunity, the great calling and the great redemption.

Let this be your understanding.

CHAPTER 7

THE INITIATION

As revealed to
Marshall Vian Summers
on June 28, 2011
in Boulder, Colorado

While the world goes about its daily affairs, the Messenger must proclaim. He must proclaim God's New Revelation, for it holds the key to so many people's lives and future.

It will initiate their calling, their greater calling, which could not be initiated by any other teaching or any other reality.

It is here to prepare the world for the great change that is coming, the Great Waves of change—the great environmental, economic and political change—which are far greater than what people anticipate today.

There are many people waiting for the New Revelation, for they have not found this Initiation in the religions of the past, in the traditions of the world. They have not been able to find the deeper connection through love, through work, through any other activity. They have been waiting so long. So long have they been waiting for the Revelation.

For them, it is not merely a teaching or a phenomenon. For them, it is not merely something to speculate about or to contend with or to deny and reject. To them, the Proclamation is not outrageous or unusual. It is the perfect thing.

It is their Initiation. It holds their calling, speaking down the Ancient Corridors of their minds, speaking to a part of them they barely know, but which is the center of their Being and their presence in the world.

For them, this is the greatest moment though they may not understand its full meaning or what it will require in the future. For them, this is what they have been waiting for.

They were sent into the world to be at a time of great transition. They were sent into the world to be a part of building a new future. Their connection is more to the future than to the past. They are the children of the future.

What has occurred before, what has been revealed before, may be inspiring or beneficial to them, but it does not hold their Initiation. It does not hold their greater calling. These things do not contain what they have been looking for and waiting for, for so very long. It is their destiny, you see.

You cannot change that which was put in place before you came into the world. Though the events of the day and of the year change your circumstances and alter your opportunities, your destiny is still the same.

You may fight with this. You may contend with this. You may try to replace it with great projects, great romances, great endeavors or any number of distractions and fantasies, but you cannot alter what was put within you before you came.

How it will occur, if it will occur, where it will occur may all be altered and is being altered by the changing circumstances of the world and by the shifting allegiances within people and their condition and their environment and so forth.

If it is your destiny to receive the New Revelation, then you cannot find your calling anywhere else. Try as you may. Be resistant. Deny it. Stand apart. Try to find fault with it. Try to belittle it. Try to keep it at bay. But you cannot alter the fact that it holds your destiny.

Your mind may speculate. Your mind will question. Your mind will think it is ridiculous; it cannot be. But your heart will know. Your soul will be activated.

It is like the Voice that spoke to you before you came into the world, preparing you to enter this difficult and challenging environment. It is that Voice—like that Voice, like Our Voice—that brings the connection alive, that restores the primary focus and meaning of your life.

But at the moment of Initiation, you will not understand. It will be so confusing. So different it is from your goals and your ideas and your notions about yourself and what you are doing in the world.

And all of a sudden, it is like you are struck with lightning, and for a moment in the darkness, everything is illuminated. And you see the truth about your life and how far you really are from your greater purpose and calling, adrift as if you were on a raft in the ocean, carried about by the winds and the waves of the world.

But God has found you as you are drifting in the vastness of the seas, found you. Like a tiny speck on the surface of the ocean, you have been found. You have been found by the Revelation.

No matter what your circumstances or state of mind, the Calling will speak to you, for it represents your destiny. It is not someone else's destiny. You need not worry about them. It is your destiny.

You may say, "What about other people? What about my spouse? What about my children? What about my dear friend?"

But God has found the speck on the ocean, and that speck is you.

This is the Initiation. Mysterious it is. You cannot comprehend it with the intellect. You cannot control what it means or what it will lead you to do. It is beyond your control because God is beyond your control.

Your great ideas, your firm beliefs, they all appear to be shallow and weak in the face of the Presence. Your arguments are hollow. Your rejection is without true emotion. Your denial is insincere. Your refusal lacks conviction. Because it is your Initiation.

And once the Initiation has been recognized, after some struggle, the journey of preparation stretches out before you. The Steps to Knowledge stretch out before you. The reclamation of your true life and all that that will require of you, and your current circumstances and obligations, are set out before you, step by step.

You cannot get to your purpose from where you are because you are adrift, and you have not found your safe harbor. You have not found the sight of land where your life is meant to be.

What a time this is then to be struck by the Revelation. Momentary it will seem, but all of a sudden, everything begins to feel different. You have had an experience that stands in contrast to your normal experiences, and this begins to create a contrast that you will carry forth with you. For nothing you can do on your own can compete with this. It is bigger than any experience that you have ever tried to have. It is greater than any goal you have ever set for yourself.

You feel frightened and overwhelmed, confused, but it is okay. It is natural. To have your life so suddenly change, certainly would create confusion and disorientation. It would certainly be disillusioning to your current obsessions and distractions.

Once God has made God's mark upon you, then it is not like you can erase it from your life or cover it up or make it go away or explain it or rationalize it to yourself so that its power is diminished. You are going to contend with the Revelation for you?

It is not by accident that you happened to come across or even hear about the New Revelation. All the forces of Heaven that support you have been trying to get you to this point of recognition and to keep you from destroying your life in the process, to limit the damage you have already done and the waste you have already created so that you would be available and be able to respond.

The Initiation may make you feel helpless and confused, highly uncertain. You might even think it is a great misfortune. But from the position and perspective of Heaven, you are the blessed amongst the few, a person who has been given the greatest opportunity. So what if it means changing your life and circumstances? What is that compared to who you are and why you have been sent?

Significant to you, yes, at this moment and meaningful perhaps to others who are involved with you. But you have been given a greater opportunity, and even more than an opportunity—a calling.

Once this Initiation has occurred, your journey will change, perhaps imperceptibly at the beginning, but something has altered the course of your life. You will never really be the same. Even if you spend your life denying and rejecting what has occurred, you will never be the same.

You will never be happy with simple pleasures alone. You will never be content with your former goals or distractions, hobbies or interests. Something has changed.

From Heaven's viewpoint, it is a great blessing. Finally, your life has a possibility of being redeemed. But to you it may seem very different in the moment.

You must then cleave to the Revelation if that is your Initiation, and you will know if it is at the center of your Being. It is not an intellectual discussion with yourself. It is not a rational process. Human rationality is merely a coping mechanism to deal with an uncertain and unpredictable world. It is appropriate in certain circumstances and hopeless in others.

It is important that you know of the Messenger because if the Initiation occurs while he is in the world, then your opportunity becomes greater and more significant. It would be a great misfortune for you to miss him while he is here.

The Revelation only comes every few centuries, or perhaps once in a millennium, and you happen to be here at that time. From Heaven's perspective, that is a great blessing, a great opportunity.

But who can recognize the Messenger? He appears to be very average. He is not sensational looking. He does not hold a great position in the world. He will disappear into the masses of people. He will walk amongst them. No one will recognize him, except perhaps for those who have been struck by the Revelation.

THE INITIATION

For those who meet with him, he may not reveal his true purpose and work in the world with them, depending on who they are. How can it be that someone would not see this? How could it be that someone of this great importance in the world would go unrecognized by the people who are standing next to him?

It is the predicament of the world. Everyone has the eyes to see and the ears to hear, but they are looking in a different way, and they are trying to hear what is in their mind and what confirms what is in their mind and not what exists in reality.

So they look, but they do not see. And they listen, but they do not hear. They stand next to the Messenger, but they do not recognize that they are standing next to the most important person in the entire world at this time.

He will never say this about himself. He is far too humble for this, so it must be said for him.

It is like centuries ago. You were having tea at a table with Muhammad, but you did not know who he was. Well, he looks like anyone else. He is not radiating the Presence. He is not so magnificent or so omnipotent that everyone around him is swooned by his presence. He is just a man, dressed traditionally, just a man. There he is. I see him now. He is over here. Nothing special. He had to preach hard to even get people to listen to him. So blind was everyone around him, only a few could see. Such is the dilemma and the burden of the Messenger at any time of Revelation.

The Initiation begins with impact. It begins with dissatisfaction and the recognition that you are searching, that you are not content with what you have and where you are and with what you are doing because this does not represent who you are and why you came here.

Those who think they are contented have not yet reached deep enough within themselves to realize they are falling far short of where they need to be and what they need to be doing.

The goal is not happiness but preparation, readiness, contact, reunion and ultimately contribution to the world, wherever it may be appropriate for the individual. That is why the pursuit of happiness is so deceiving because the Revelation will make you uncomfortable. It will challenge you.

Do you think God is going to come and comfort you when you are sent into the world to do something that you are not doing now and have no hope of doing unless something greater is given to you, unless you are called out of the crowd, unless your journey is altered by the Power of Heaven?

You will just be a speck on the ocean, unknown to yourself, unknown to others. Even if you have a great position and have acquired wealth and stature in society, the empty nature of your life will be pervasive unless you have found your greater work and are doing it to the best of your ability.

Those who do this experience a satisfaction and a sense of value and power that are lost to everyone else, no matter what they proclaim for themselves.

God's New Revelation will clarify the nature of human spirituality, which has been overlaid by culture, by convention and by political manipulation.

It will make it clear that you are born with two minds—a worldly mind that is conditioned by the world and a deeper mind within you that is still connected to God. It will make it clear that the intellect has limits, and beyond these limits you must go beneath the surface of the mind.

It will make it clear that you cannot fulfill yourself apart from your greater work and destiny and that all the pleasures you seek will be temporary and will not satisfy the deeper need of your soul.

It will make it clear that you are living at a time of great change, where humanity's isolation in the universe will come to an end and where the Great Waves of change will strike the world—a time of great upheaval and uncertainty, a time for the Revelation to occur.

People may want many things of the Messenger—hoping for dispensations, for miracles, hoping to believe in someone supernatural, hoping to have their lives be enriched by his presence and his work.

They will be disappointed, as have the previous Messengers disappointed many people. That is why Messengers are denied, rejected, avoided and, in some cases, destroyed because the people do not get what they want. They only receive what they truly need.

What people want and the Will of Heaven are so very different. But if in truth you could discern your deeper requirements for life beyond survival and acquiring the simple things that are necessary for stability and safety in the world, you would see that what you want and the Will of Heaven are really the same. But this recognition would happen only at a very deep state of self-honesty for the individual.

It is unlikely you have found this quite yet. But you who are hearing Our words have come to the point where Initiation can occur. You must listen with your heart, not with your judgment and your ideas and all of the requirements you think are required for the Revelation to be real and to be meaningful to you, as if you could determine such things.

Even in people's misery, they still do not have the humility to recognize that they cannot establish the terms of engagement regarding their primary relationship with the Creator and with the Will of Heaven.

Your religious beliefs cannot really do this because it happens beyond the realm of belief. Belief will not get you into your Ancient Home, your Heavenly state, because belief is too weak, too temporary. When you leave this world, you will not have any beliefs. They all pass with the body. You will just be there, you as you really are.

Your Spiritual Family will receive you and ask you if you achieved certain things, and in that moment, without the burden and the blinding effect of your beliefs, it will be clear as day that you either did or did not fulfill these primary functions. And there is no condemnation if you should decline. It just means your work is not yet done.

You have to work your way back into Heaven, you see. You have to serve the separated world, the separated universe. You have to work your way back, through contribution and through self-development. You cannot return to your Ancient Home as a miserable, conflicted, contentious, grievous person. Heaven would seem like Hell to you, if that were the case.

God does not simply dispense with all these problems because God did not create them. They have to be uncreated. God has given you the power of Knowledge, the deeper intelligence, and a greater calling to erase the tragedy of your former life and existence and to restore to you the dignity and the purpose that are yours to claim and the purpose that is yours to serve.

THE INITIATION

It all begins with the Initiation. If it is to be true and efficacious, it begins with the Initiation. That is where God sets the terms of engagement and establishes the beginning of your real journey Home.

You cannot take yourself back to your true state because you do not know the way. You cannot simply follow a prescription from someone else because the engagement with Knowledge and the Presence must occur somewhere along the line, or this is an intellectual enterprise and not a journey of the soul.

Time is short for the world. There is no time to spend decades and centuries perfecting yourself or trying to work out your dilemmas. The Calling is for now. The hour is late.

This will be pressure for you if you can respond, but the pressure will shorten the time it takes for you to respond and to prepare. And that is a great blessing, for time equals suffering for those who cannot respond.

The gift is within you, but you cannot unlock the door. You do not have the key. You cannot discover your deeper nature because you do not yet have the whole picture. You are not yet in relationship with your Source because your deeper nature is the relationship with your Source. How could it be you would ever find it living in Separation, lost in the oceans of the world?

This is the gift of Heaven—that your life can be redeemed. But you must allow the pathway to be presented to you.

You must respond to the Revelation. If you have not responded to God's previous Revelations, then you are waiting for the New Revelation.

At some point, at a moment of despair or disillusionment, you will feel a deeper stirring within you. And you will recognize that you have come for a greater purpose that you have not yet discovered, but which awaits you, waiting for the moment where your life is being called.

CHAPTER 8

THE BLESSING

As revealed to
Marshall Vian Summers
on April 20, 2007
in Istanbul, Turkey

The Blessing is upon humanity, for this is a time of Revelation. This is the time when humanity is given a great gift, a great gift to give it purpose and direction facing the difficult and uncertain times ahead.

This is the time in which humanity receives a greater understanding of its spirituality, a call for its unity and cooperation and its destiny—both within this world and beyond this world within a Greater Community of intelligent life in the universe.

For humanity has reached a great threshold, a threshold from which there is no turning back. It is a threshold unlike any threshold that humanity as a whole has ever reached before.

Now you must become a people of the world—not just people of one nation or tribe or group. For you are emerging into a Greater Community of intelligent life, where all whom you may encounter and all who watch you now will consider you people of the world.

Here you are entering a greater panorama of life, and you are entering a competitive environment in the universe unlike anything you could even imagine. How you conduct yourself here, how you conduct your relations with each other, how you regard your position in the universe—all have tremendous weight in determining your future and how your destiny within this Greater Community will be fulfilled and even if it can be fulfilled.

You have reached the great threshold where you have the power to destroy the life-sustaining resources of this world and to set humanity into a permanent state of decline.

You have the power to compete with each other, as you have always competed, to drive humanity into this great state of decline. And [yet] you have the power to choose another way, a way out of a dilemma that will only become more difficult and intractable as time goes on.

What you as an individual will do, what you as part of a larger group and a larger nation will do, will determine which of these two great choices you will make. If you continue to conduct yourself as you have in the past, as is your habit, then your future is predictable and is extremely grave.

Yet if you choose another way, then you can establish a new beginning, and you can express a greater promise that resides within the hearts of all who dwell here.

The Blessing here is to call forth this greater promise. It begins within the individual, of course, but it extends beyond the human family.

This has called a New Message from God into the world, for only a New Message from God can contain such a Blessing. Only it has the power to call forth the greater wisdom and the greater compassion that the Creator of all life has placed within each person.

There is no individual, there is no philosophy, there is no school of thought that can generate such a calling. It must come from the Creator of all life. It must come from the God of the entire Greater

Community—the One God, the One Source, whose Angels watch over the world, but whose Power extends beyond what humanity can even imagine.

God has placed within each person the seed of Knowledge so that this calling may be responded to. This Knowledge is a greater intelligence within each person waiting to be discovered, but its whole existence is in relationship to the Creator of all life.

It is not a resource that you can use for yourself to enrich yourself or to gain advantage over others. For Knowledge will not do these things. Its purpose and its reality are to respond to the Creator of all life and to respond to the great calling that is going out as humanity continues to approach this great threshold in its existence.

For it is at this great turning point that humanity will choose success or failure in the face of immense difficulty in the world and in the face of opposing and competing forces from the Greater Community itself who seek to take advantage of a struggling and divided humanity.

Many people around the world are feeling a great discomfort, a great uneasiness about the condition of the world and have grave concern for its future and for the future of humanity. They sense and feel and know that they are living at a time of great power, a time that will determine the fate and the outcome for humanity. This is not an intellectual understanding as much as it is a visceral experience, a powerful recognition, an innate sense of awareness—all of which come from Knowledge within them.

There is no escaping this great time, this great turning point. There is no more losing yourself in your fantasies and your individual pursuits. For if you enter this great time, this great threshold and this time of Revelation blind and self-obsessed, you will not be able to see, to know and to prepare.

You may pray to God for deliverance. You may pray to God for the Blessing. But the Blessing and the deliverance have already been placed within you—within Knowledge within you—awaiting the time when you would have the maturity, when you would have the need, when you would have the understanding that such a power within you must be called upon, must be followed, must be honored above all else.

For this is your relationship with God, and the urgency you feel within yourself is the Calling of God—the Calling to awaken, to become aware and to respond.

Do not think that without your participation your life will have a greater possibility. Do not think that you can sleep through the greatest event in human history and expect to benefit from the changing circumstances around you. And do not think that you can find peace and equanimity by trying to overlook the great times in which you live. For there will be no peace and equanimity there. There will be no comfort and consolation there.

You are living in a time of Revelation. You are living at a time when humanity faces its greatest threshold, its greatest challenges, its greatest danger and yet its one great opportunity to establish human cooperation and unity in the face of grave and dire circumstances.

To see this and to know this for yourself, you must be able to overcome your own denial. You must be able to overcome the conditioning of your culture. You must be able to overcome your own preferences and your own seeking for escape. Perhaps you think this is not possible, but the power of Knowledge within you will enable you to do this and enable others to do this.

The Calling now is going forth. A New Message from God is in the world. The Messenger is in the world. He is now prepared to present the New Message. It contains the Blessing. It contains the Warning. It contains the Preparation.

It is not here to replace the world's religions but to establish and reinforce their common ground, to enlighten them and to give them strength and purpose so that they may have a future—both within the world and within the Greater Community of life into which humanity is now emerging.

In the face of this great threshold, your governments will not have an answer. Your philosophers will not have an answer. Perhaps people will see part of the solution and attempt to express that, and that is necessary, but the answer must come from a greater power within you and a Greater Power beyond you.

For what will be required is a great shift in human understanding and a change in human behavior. These things must be necessitated by a Greater Power and by a greater response within you and within people all around the world. Not everyone will have to respond, but enough people in many places will need to experience this calling and this response.

The time is short. It is not time now to become listless or indecisive. There is no luxury in remaining ignorant and foolish in the face of the Great Waves of change.

For there is a Greater Darkness in the world. It is a Darkness more profound and more consequential than anything that humanity has ever faced before.

It enters the world at a time of great vulnerability for the human family, as you face a world in decline and as you face the great decision before you as to whether humanity will choose the path of self-destruction—a path born of competition, conflict and war—or whether the other path, the other way, will be recognized and claimed and required and expressed, a path towards cooperation and unity in the face of great danger.

Many people around the world are beginning to see the evidence of this great danger, but many people are still asleep, dreaming of their own personal fulfillment, unaware and inattentive to the Great Waves of change that are already washing over the world.

It will therefore be necessary for those who can respond to respond fully—to recognize the great threat, to hear the great warning and to receive the great Blessing from the Creator of all life.

There is an answer for humanity, but it is not an answer that humanity can invent for itself entirely. For the answer must have the power to call people into a greater service to one another. It must have the power to overcome and override the psychological, the social and the political ideologies and tendencies that continue to cast humanity in opposition to itself. It must be a power great enough to incite compassion, tolerance and forgiveness in the human family.

It is not simply a set of ideas. It is the power of redemption. It is a calling from God and a response from God's Creation—a response within people, a response within you.

Therefore, receive the Blessing. You will not be able to understand it intellectually, but you can feel it and know that it is genuine. You can feel the response stirring within yourself.

Honor this response and allow it to emerge in your awareness. Allow it to lead you forward. It is the guidance that the Creator is providing for you. It has been sleeping within you as you have been sleeping around it.

Now it must awaken, for the time for its emergence has come. Now you must look out into the world with clear and objective eyes. Now you must set aside the childish and foolish preoccupations that can only keep you weak and blind and vulnerable.

This is a time of Revelation. Such times only come very rarely—at great turning points for the human family, at great moments of opportunity where the Creator of all life can give humanity a greater Wisdom and Knowledge and a new infusion of inspiration and spiritual power.

This is your time. This is the time you have come for. For you did not come all the way into this world with the assistance of the Angelic Host simply to be a consumer here—simply to build a nest for yourself, simply to enrich yourself and to struggle with others for this enrichment.

Though this may be the reality of your life here at this moment, it is not your greater reality, which is to bring something more precious into the world, something the world cannot give itself, and to allow this gift to reshape your life and redirect your life in service to humanity and in service to life within this world.

Yet a purpose must be activated by a greater calling and a greater set of circumstances. Therefore, do not shrink from the Great Waves of change that are coming, but face them. You will be frightened and uncertain in their shadow, but their reality will also ignite a spiritual power within you, and this spiritual power will come forth because of the Calling, because of the Blessing.

For God is calling all who are asleep now to awaken from their dreams of misery and fulfillment, to respond to this great time and to prepare to render the gifts that they were sent into the world to give to a struggling humanity—a humanity whose future now will be largely determined within the few years to come. This is the Blessing.

You may pray to God for many things. You may ask to be preserved. You may pray for opportunity and advantage. You may pray for the well-being of your family members and loved ones. But there is no greater response that you could give and there is no greater gift that could be given than the Blessing. For the Blessing responds to a far greater question that comes from within you, from the need of your soul. It is a communication far beyond the the reach of the intellect or the needs of the moment. It provides for far more than you have learned to ask for.

It is a way. It is a path. It is an awareness. It is a journey. It is a mountain to climb. That is the Blessing.

That is what will rearrange your life and give it meaning. That is what will organize your thinking and give you an escape from ambivalence and chaos. This, regardless of your circumstances, will bring the Blessing into your life so that others can see it and feel it and respond to it. It is intangible. It is ineffable. Yet it has the power to bring all the greater rewards into the human family.

It is only the Blessing that can prepare and protect humanity. It is only the Blessing that will give you the pathway through the uncertain and difficult times ahead. And it is only the Blessing that can prepare you for the Greater Darkness that is in the world—the Greater Darkness that has the power to determine the future of every person and every future person in this world.

This is a time calling for human unity and human power and human wisdom to come to the fore. For you now face competition from beyond the world, as well as disastrous circumstances within the world. It is a set of circumstances that are unprecedented in all of humanity's existence.

Think not that such a reality is in some distant future or that it is not upon you now. Unless you can see the great challenge, you will not feel the great need. If you cannot feel the great need, you will not recognize the Blessing. You will not feel the need for the Blessing. You will not see that without the Blessing, humanity will enter a period of prolonged decline, with grave and immensely difficult circumstances.

God understands humanity's predicament even if humanity cannot recognize it itself. God knows the need of your soul even if you cannot yet fully feel it within yourself. God knows what is coming for humanity and is calling for humanity to prepare—to become awake and aware—to prepare.

God's Will and human decision are not the same. Therefore, the outcome is up to people. The Creator has already given the great endowment of Knowledge. The Angels watch over the world. But the outcome is in the hands of the people.

People can choose—as many other races in the Greater Community have chosen through time immemorial—to fail, to decline, to fall under the persuasion and domination of other forces. This has happened countless times both within your world and within the immense vastness of the universe.

What God wills and what people choose and want for themselves are not the same. And that is the problem. That is the conundrum. That is what creates the great Separation. This is what disables you from following Knowledge within yourself. This is what keeps people blind, engendering foolish and destructive behavior. Therefore, if you can recognize the problem, you put yourself in a position to recognize the solution.

The Calling must come from God. The answer is within Knowledge within you and Knowledge within everyone. There is no competition or conflict between this Knowledge, as it exists in everyone. How different it is from your theories and ideas, your prescriptions and your societies' prescriptions.

In the end, humanity must take courageous action and make difficult decisions. But the Calling is there.

Your decisions and your actions must follow the Blessing and not precede it. Allow yourself to receive the gift of the Blessing and then, step by step, you will know what to do—what series of actions you must undertake, the thresholds that you must pass through and the change that you must bring about in your own thinking and your own circumstances. Action and understanding follow the Blessing.

To give, you must first receive. To know, your eyes must first be open. To have the power and the courage to respond, you must see the need and feel the greatness of the times in which you live.

You must prepare your mind and your emotions. You must prepare yourself to receive the Blessing and to experience the greater response within you, the great calling to Knowledge within you. You must allow this Knowledge to emerge slowly, without trying to control it or dominate it or manipulate it in any way.

In this way, the Blessing takes hold within you and grows forth within you. For the Blessing is not a momentary thing. It is not something you experience like a flash of lightning. It does not illuminate the landscape at night for a second only.

It begins a process of emergence. It begins a process of renewal. It begins the process of redemption that can direct and fulfill the remainder of your life here. Such is the great need of humanity, and such is the great need of your soul and of all who dwell here.

May the power of the Blessing now, and may the gravity of your situation, reveal themselves to you most powerfully. And may you pass through the initial feelings of fear, insecurity and inadequacy in order to respond and to allow the response to happen within your life, as it will do today, tomorrow and each day to follow. For this is the time of Revelation. And you are here at the time of Revelation.

CHAPTER 9

LIVING AT A TIME
OF REVELATION

As revealed to
Marshall Vian Summers
on September 27, 2011
in Leadville, Colorado

For the first time in the history of this world, you are able to witness the process of Revelation. Aided with modern technology, the whole process is being recorded so there can be no mistake in future interpretations, as has been so often the case in the past.

It is not merely the Revelation itself that is significant. It is the process of Revelation itself—to be able to hear the Voice, so similar to that which spoke to the Jesus, the Buddha and the Muhammad and many other great teachers, both known and unrecognized in the history of this world.

This is a unique opportunity and a profound education that can clarify many errors in religious thinking and cast all of God's previous Revelations in a new and much clearer light.

For in the history of this world and all worlds, the process of Revelation is the same. An individual is selected and sent into the world. When they reach a certain stage in their development and maturity, they are called out of normal circumstances, called to a great rendezvous, a great encounter with the Angelic Presence that oversees that particular world. Then they are called into a greater service and prepared for a greater service, prepared to bring something new and revolutionary into the world.

This is not merely a refinement of past understandings or past beliefs. It is something really new and revolutionary. It is not merely an improvement or an enhancement or a new perspective on something that has already been provided and is well established. It is a new threshold.

You have the opportunity to witness the Revelation and the process of Revelation and the clarification of the Revelation and the meaning of the Revelation for your life and for the whole world.

For it is a Message for the whole world, not just for one tribe or one people or one nation or one region. It is not a revision of what has been given before. It is not a reaction to what has been given before. It is not adjunct to any teaching or theology that exists in the world. It is something new and revolutionary. It represents a great threshold and a great challenge for the human family.

Wherever you are living, whatever nation you are in, whatever your circumstances, you are living at a time of Revelation, as great as any time of Revelation in the past.

Your ability to respond to the Revelation will determine your readiness, your openness, your honesty and your sincerity. For everything that is false, everything that is disingenuous, everything that is corrupt or mistaken is revealed in the Light of the Revelation.

Who can receive a new Messenger from God? Who will reject him? How will people respond? Will they respond at all?

All is revealed at the time of Revelation—the value of one's religious understanding, the purity of one's religious faith, the clarity and honesty of one's approach, the openness of one's heart and mind. All of these are revealed at the time of Revelation. And you are now living at a time of Revelation.

One man has been prepared and sent into the world. There can be no others who can make such a claim, for Heaven knows who is chosen and who is not. Those who choose themselves and elect themselves, they cannot bring a New Revelation into the world. They do not have the power or the clarity, and most importantly, they do not have the Revelation itself.

Everything is revealed at a time of Revelation.

The process of Revelation is so very different from the stories and the fantasies and the miracles that people ascribe to such events, such seminal events in human history that have been glorified and escalated way out of the ordinary to try to give greater prominence and significance to the teachings that emerged from such great events.

But these great events all have humble beginnings. They are not grand and sensational. They are not filled with miracles and extraordinary events where everyone stands in awe. That is the difference between reality and human invention.

But the Revelation is extraordinary. It is rare. For God only sends a New Message into the world perhaps once in a millennium, at a time of great threshold, challenge and difficulty for the human family; at a time of great opportunity and great need, where a New Revelation must be given, not simply further commentary on what has been provided before.

It is this then that must reach beyond the ideas and beliefs of the listener into a deeper part of them, a deeper intelligence within them, a part of them that is still connected to God, the part of them that We call Knowledge.

You cannot fool Knowledge. There is no error in perception at this level. But alas so few people have gained this state of mind, this deeper connection, sufficiently that they can see clearly and follow Knowledge, which represents the direction of God's Will and Purpose in the world.

The Revelation before you is the greatest and largest Revelation ever given to humanity, for it speaks to a literate world, a world of global communications, a world of greater sophistication and a world of escalating and profound need, confusion and misery.

It is the first great Revelation to be given to a world community, to a literate population. And that is why it must speak now with greater clarity, greater emphasis, greater sophistication and complexity.

For you cannot be a child and face what you will be facing in the world and beyond. You cannot be simply a blind follower and prepare yourself for the Great Waves of change that are coming to the world or for humanity's encounter with intelligent life in the universe—the greatest and most consequential event in history.

You cannot worship God and think that you are fulfilling your destiny here, for each of you has been sent into the world for a greater purpose that is connected to the evolution of the world and to the reality of human need around you.

Only Knowledge within you knows what this means specifically and what must be done to prepare you for it and what must be achieved through you and through others whom you will naturally associate with in light of a greater purpose.

The Revelation is not here to create a pantheon of gods or fantastic stories that seem incredulous and difficult to believe. It is not here to make you into servants of God as much as it is to encourage you to represent the Divine Will and Purpose, which only Knowledge within you can enable you to do.

It is a great Revelation for a future that will be unlike the past— for a world in decline; a world of declining resources; a world of environmental destruction; a world where it will be more difficult to take care of people, to provide food, water, medicine and energy around the world; a world of greater danger and contention; and beyond this a world that is facing intervention from races in the universe who are here to take advantage of human weakness and expectations.

Therefore, the Message is very powerful, but it must be very clarifying. And the Messenger must proclaim this and also be able to teach what it means. This is something that has required decades of preparation. It has taken the Messenger decades to even receive the New Message from God, it is so vast and inclusive.

The Messenger must be a man without position in the world, but he must be well educated and very compassionate. He must be simple and humble. He must speak clearly but in terms that everyone can understand. He must demonstrate through his life the value of his Message and the significance of living and learning a New Revelation.

He is not perfect, but none of the Messengers have ever been perfect. He is not going to produce miracles for the masses because none of the Messengers have ever really done that. He is here to open the door to a deeper experience of the Divine Presence and Power in the lives of people everywhere—rich and poor, north and south, east and west, in all nations, in all religions. He is not here to replace the world's religions, but to provide a greater clarity and relevance to them.

For humanity must prepare for the Great Waves of change that are coming to the world if human civilization is to survive and to be stable and to be a foundation for humanity's greatest accomplishments in the future.

Humanity also must be prepared and educated about life in the universe, to the extent that you will need to understand in order to determine how you will respond to the presence of an intervention in your own world.

None of the world's religions can prepare you for these things, for they were born of an earlier epoch, and though they are immensely important for humanity, it will take a New Revelation from God to save human civilization, to bring greater unity between the world's religions, to bring an end to war and conflict so that humanity may prepare itself for the great challenges to come.

You cannot be anchored in the past and understand the Revelation of the future. You cannot be adamant about your religious views and comprehend how God will speak again and why God has spoken again and what it will mean for you and for others. Your heart cannot be closed, or you will not hear and you will not see.

You must love humanity enough to value such a Revelation and to live according to what it teaches, to receive the power that it provides, the grace and the compassion that it emphasizes.

The Messenger is facing a very hazardous journey ahead, for there will be much resistance to the New Revelation, as there has always been great resistance in the past to God's Revelations in the world, whenever and wherever they were given.

He will not be speaking in every town. He will not be present at every event. He will only speak here and there. But his Message will be broadcast to the world, and the Revelation will be presented to the world with its own commentary, its own directives, its own clarification. It is not something that will be left up to future scholars and individuals to interpret, to comment upon, for that has proven to be hazardous and unfortunate in the past.

That is why the Revelation is so explicit and so repetitive. That is why it is so clarifying, to minimize the possibility of human error, misperception and misunderstanding.

It restores to the individual the power of Knowledge, which was only the privilege of the elite and the elect before. It speaks of the deeper conscience of humanity, the conscience that was established before you even came here, to be your guide and counsel in all things important.

The Messenger must not be worshipped. He is not a god. None of the Messengers were gods. They were Messengers—half human, half holy—representing both realities, the reality of the world and the reality of the Ancient Home from which you have all come and to which you will all return eventually.

His presence will clarify what must be clarified. His voice will speak to the minds and the hearts of those who can hear. He will speak to the needs of the world and the needs of the heart and the soul. He brings not only the answers, but the answer itself. For God has placed a greater intelligence and mind within each person, but this is not known of to any great extent in the world, save but by a few.

It will not simply be human technology and human ingenuity that will be able to prepare you adequately for the future, for the Greater Community itself. It will have to be something much more profound and essential to your nature and your Being. The Messenger will speak of these things.

This is all part of the Revelation, you see. God does not give you an answer for the day or an answer for tomorrow, but an answer for all days and all situations.

God does not have to direct your life, for the Lord of all the universes is not engaged with you in this way. God is more intelligent. God has put Knowledge within you, a perfect guiding intelligence to be discerned from all the other voices and impulses, desires and fears in your mind.

The Revelation has provided the Steps to Knowledge, the pathway for gaining access to that which is the greatest endowment that God could ever give to humanity or to any emerging or advanced race in the universe.

Your understanding of the Divine now must be taken into a greater panorama of life. Your understanding cannot be anchored in the past, but must be flexible and be able to adapt to the future, as greater and greater change occurs within you and around you. Your Lord now must be the Lord of the universes, a Lord of a billion, billion, billion races and many more.

This is part of the Revelation for humanity, so very different and more expansive than any Revelation that has ever been given. With this, you will value all of the Revelations and gain wisdom from them all.

If you are a devout Christian, your Christianity will now grow and become more expansive. If you are a devout Muslim, your faith and practice will now grow and become more expansive. If you are a practicing Buddhist or of the Jewish faith or any religious pathway, it will all become enlarged by the New Revelation. The Messenger will speak of these things. The Revelation speaks of these things.

And for the first time, you will hear the Voice of Revelation. It was never possible to record this previously for obvious reasons, but now you will be able to hear the Voice of Revelation. It is a wondrous thing, but it is also a challenge for you, for if you cannot hear this, if you cannot recognize this, then you must face your own impediments. You might criticize, deny and avoid this, but that only shows your weakness and your limitations.

What more does God have to do for you? If you cannot receive the Revelation, what can God do for you? God has given an answer to the whole world and to you individually—to your faith, to your tradition, to your religion, to your culture and to your nation. Do you want favors? Do you want dispensations? Do you want to be relieved of the difficulties of life? Do you want to be pampered? Do you want miracles at every turn? Do you want to be on some kind of welfare to Heaven, as if you were helpless and impotent in the world?

God gives you strength through Knowledge and calls upon Knowledge through the New Revelation.

It is not God who will save the world, but it is the people who were sent here to save the world that will do it. And they will play their small but significant role, and it will be greater than they understand. And it will be different from their personal goals and ambitions. And it will redeem them and revive them, returning to them the strength and Power of Heaven, which is embodied in Knowledge within them, deep beneath the surface of the mind.

You have the opportunity to understand the process of Revelation. And if you can understand this, you will see what a miracle it really is. And you will not turn the Messenger into a god, but accord him the respect and deference that he deserves. And you will be honest in your approach—not to dismiss or to disdain the Revelation, but to hear it, to experience it and to apply it to your life sufficiently so that you may comprehend its greater purpose and meaning for you.

People want God to do many things for them—save them from calamity, give them opportunities, heal the sick, overturn corrupt and oppressive governments, make them rich, make them happy, make them content or be at peace.

But what people want and what God wills are not the same, not at first. For the real needs of your heart resonate with the Will of the Creator, but the real needs of your heart and soul may be something that is not within your awareness yet. A deeper honesty will take you there.

God has provided the power of Knowledge and with it the pathway and the engagement with life that will redeem the individual. This serves everyone, even the wicked, even the poorest of the poor.

Here there are no heroes and masters. There are only those who are stronger with Knowledge who can demonstrate its grace and power in the world.

How very different this is from what people are taught to think and to believe. But thoughts and beliefs are at the surface of the mind. Beneath the surface is the great opening to your true nature and to the power of Knowledge.

You do not yet realize how important and central this is to your life. That is why the Revelation must provide clarification of what religion really is and means, what spirituality really is and means, and how all true spiritual practices are in essence steps to Knowledge.

But it is difficult to find this in the religions of the world, so overlaid they have become with ritual, tradition, commentary and misinterpretation. For many, they have become rigid beliefs; for others, a consolation only. Their true power can only be found within them with a great teacher and a wise guide.

Humanity does not have time for this now, for the hour is late. This is not merely for certain individuals to take a greater journey in life. It is for the whole human family to prepare in the most practical and essential ways for the great change that is coming to the world, and that is already beginning to strike the shores and to overwhelm the cities, to cast nations in conflict with one another, to darken your skies, to pollute your rivers, to threaten the very resources you depend upon every day.

The Revelation is not here to frighten you, but to empower you; to give you strength, courage and determination; to give you compassion and tolerance; to give you the power of Knowledge, which is the source of your real strength and integrity.

The world is changed, but people have not changed with it. The Great Waves are coming, but people do not know. Intervention is occurring in the world, but people are unaware or perhaps think it is a wonderful thing.

It will take a Revelation from the Creator of all life to prepare humanity, to awaken humanity and to strengthen and unite humanity so that it may have a greater future and survive the great challenge to its freedom and its destiny.

There is so much to learn. There are so many things to be set aside, so many things to be questioned, so many things to be reconsidered. A Revelation from God brings all of this. It is a great challenge to the recipient and to the people who are so blessed to receive it.

And while the Messenger is in the world, you have this great opportunity to hear him, to consider his words and the meaning of his presence in the world at this time.

It will be a great shock to many. It will be resisted by many. It will be received by many.

But it will take a great shock to awaken humanity to the reality of its situation and to the circumstances for which it must prepare. It will take the shock of Revelation. It will take the shock of the future. It will take the reality of this present moment and the realization that one is not living the life they were sent here to live and the recognition that your ideas alone cannot prepare you for greater things, that you must have the power of Knowledge, which is the strength of Heaven that has been given to you.

This is the meaning of Revelation. It is not merely a Revelation of ideas. It is a Revelation of experience. It is a Revelation of one's true nature, origin and destiny.

May your eyes be open for this. May your heart be receptive. May your ideas be flexible enough to be reconsidered. And may you realize that you are here to serve a greater purpose, which you yourself cannot invent or direct. May the Revelation be yours, and through you given to others. May the Messenger be recognized and honored in his remaining time on Earth. And may this be a time of great blessing, clarification and encouragement for you who are seeking to find the greater purpose and direction of your life.

THE ASSEMBLY

As revealed to
Marshall Vian Summers
on February 16, 2013
in Boulder, Colorado

There is a great Assembly, the Angelic Presence that watches over this world and has watched over this world for a very long time.

How different this is, however, from people's notions and beliefs, the way that such great Beings have been portrayed in the past in your books on religion and in the testimony of certain people.

God is not managing the world. God is not running the climate. God is not moving the blood through your veins or pouring the waters over the cliffs or germinating the seeds in the ground—for that was all set into motion at the beginning of time.

But God has assigned a Presence to watch over the world through all of its chaotic and tragic encounters and episodes in history—watching for those individuals who show greater promise; bringing things into the world at key turning points in humanity's evolution; and sending one of their own into the world to bring a new Teaching and a new understanding to change the awareness of humanity and to alter, if possible, the course of humanity in a positive way.

Those who you honor as the great Messengers, the great Saints, the great Teachers—such as the Jesus, the Buddha and the Muhammad—come from this Assembly, you see. But when they are in the world, they are human beings. What distinguishes them is that they are here on a greater mission with a greater set of responsibilities and a greater accountability to those who sent them. Their lives are trials. Their lives are demanding. It is not a journey for the faint of heart or for those seeking pleasure and repose here on Earth.

The Assembly watches over the world—listening, waiting for those requests that are truly authentic and represent an honest appeal, particularly if they mark a turning point in a person's life, particularly if they show a greater demonstration of a desire for contact—not borne of ambition, not borne of foolishness or experimentation.

It is the signal that someone is ready to begin to awaken. Only Heaven knows what this signal is, what it sounds like, what it means and how it should be regarded.

For you here on Earth, the Assembly is like Heaven—a bridge between this world and your Ancient Home, from which you have come and to which you will return eventually.

Everyone in the world, everyone in the universe living in Separation in the physical reality, will return to their Ancient Home eventually.

But while they are here, they are prisoners to their own intentions. They are prisoners to their cultures and their nations, in a universe where freedom is so very rare. Yet each has been sent here for a greater purpose—a potential, a seed of wisdom, a possibility that, given the right circumstances and given their own honesty and awareness, a greater life can be initiated.

Every world where sentient beings have evolved or have migrated and colonized in the universe, there will be an Assembly there—a great Assembly or a small Assembly, depending on the number of individuals and the nature and conditions of that culture and nation in the universe.

It is a Plan on a scale you cannot even imagine. Your religions cannot account for it. Your theology is far too limited in scope to encompass something of this magnitude. Try as you may to interpret the signs and the symbols of life on Earth, you cannot interpret this. Your intellect was not created to interpret something on this scale.

But within you is the power of Knowledge that God has placed there—a deeper intelligence, a deeper mind. It is this mind that the Assembly is waiting for. For if this deeper mind within you can emerge within the context of your life and circumstances and be accepted and followed and received, you will begin now a new journey in life. Only in this regard can it be said that you would be born again in the world. Only in this regard would that be true and meaningful and efficacious.

Members of the Assembly will attend to certain individuals who are making a greater contribution to the world, but only if the deeper Knowledge within those individuals is sending the message—the message the Assembly is waiting for and looking for amongst those who live in Separation.

God allows you to be in Separation. God allows you to suffer. God allows you to make mistakes because that is why you have chosen Separation—to have this freedom.

But since there is no real alternative to Creation, your existence here is only partially real. It is still connected to Creation, but is a changing, evolving environment—an environment where your life is temporary and greatly challenged and greatly endangered by many things, where error and failure will be the consequence of living without this Knowledge to guide you.

God allows this to happen because you were made to be free. You are even free to try to not be who you really are. You are even that free.

But you can never succeed in Separation because Knowledge lives within you. It is the part of you that has never left God and still responds to the Power and Presence of the Lord of Creation and of Creation itself.

Think of your religious teachings in the world—the stories, the teachings, the vast array of ideas associated with these—and consider them in light of what We are saying to you here today. For We are giving you the big picture of your life. See the contrast and you will begin to see that you must embark on a new journey.

Your old ideas of religion and spirituality can only serve you to a certain degree. Beyond that, they must be set aside, for only God knows the way to return. Only God knows the meaning of your true existence and the specific purpose that has brought you into the world at this time, under these circumstances.

The intellect must bow down eventually. It can only follow when attending a greater reality. This requires humility. This requires surrendering, over time, to the power and the presence that lives within you, that can only respond to your Source.

The Assembly allows everything to happen on Earth. Unless their Presence is required and requested with the greatest sincerity, they will not interfere. Only at a great turning point, when a New Message is meant to be given to the world, will they provide humanity a new understanding, a greater awareness. And this will occur in response to great and potentially devastating change in the world. That is why the great Revelations are only given at certain critical turning points in the evolution of human civilization. They cannot be fabricated. They cannot be invented. They cannot even be imagined, though many people have tried, of course.

It is upon these that the great traditions have been built. But it is also upon these that the great traditions have not been able to follow the spirit of the Revelation that initiated their existence in the beginning. God knows that without Knowledge, people would be in error regarding these things and would make many mistakes along the way. It is the condition of living in Separation.

But once you begin to discover the power and presence of Knowledge within yourself, you begin to end the Separation within yourself— between your worldly mind and idea of yourself and the greater intelligence that lives within you, an intelligence you had before you came into the world and which you will rediscover once you leave.

This requires a great resonance with life and not merely a complex theology or philosophy. The Angelic Assembly does not respond to those things.

But at a great turning point, such as is occurring in the world today, one of their own will come into the world. One of their own will be sent to face the tribulation of being the Messenger—the great difficulty, the great mystery, the great uncertainty, the great Presence that will abide with them as they go through the process of becoming an adult human being, with yet little awareness of their greater destiny and purpose until their calling has been initiated.

No one understands the life of the Messenger, but everyone can receive the gifts of the Messenger, which are gifts that are greater than any person could ever give to the world—gifts far more long lasting, pervasive, powerful and inspiring than any person could ever create or invent. People may have compelling ideas, but nothing that can transform the life of a person in the most natural and beautiful way.

That must come from Heaven. It must come through the Assembly that interprets the Will of God. For God of the universe is far too great to be preoccupied with this world—the God of countless galaxies, dimensions and Creation beyond the physical manifestation, which is even greater, so great that there is no possibility that you could comprehend its scope and its great inclusion in life.

The Lord of a billion, billion, billion races and more is certainly beyond any theological principle that has ever been created in this world. But it is part of God's New Revelation, you see, because humanity is emerging into a Greater Community of life in the universe and must now begin to think of God in a greater panorama.

For to understand what God is doing in this world, you must understand what God is doing in the universe. And for the first time, the Revelation concerning this is being given to a humanity that stands at the threshold of space, to a humanity that stands at the threshold of destroying the environment of the world and driving itself into ruin and catastrophe. It is the greatest threshold humanity has ever faced, and the most consequential.

Everything will change and is changing even at this moment. Because of this great turning point, God has sent, through the Angelic Presence and Assembly, a New Revelation for the world—a Revelation about life in the universe and the work of God everywhere, not based upon a tribe or a region or upon a natural phenomenon or upon the limited history of a group or a nation, but upon the reality of life everywhere.

This greater panorama gives you the greatest opportunity to recognize the power and the presence that lives within you and encourages you to use your intellect to support this realization, for this is what it was created to do, and this is its highest service to you.

You will not know the names of those in the Assembly though they might provide a name at some point for some person to help them to respond. Their names are meaningless, for they are both individuals and they are one—a phenomenon you cannot comprehend with the intellect, which can only think of things of this world.

At the time of great Revelation, the Assembly speaks as one Voice. It speaks through one of its members, but they are all speaking at once, a phenomenon that you cannot really consider. It is too marvelous. It is too phenomenal. It speaks beyond your notions of reality entirely. You can only imagine individuals in the universe, but the Assembly is one and many and one, because they are so close to Heaven, you see, where the many are one, and the one are many.

Your focus in life is not to become enamored with the Assembly or to concentrate on the Assembly, for their purpose is to engage you in the reclamation of Knowledge that lives within you.

For you must be the one who chooses. You must be the one who faces the consequences and the difficulties and the blessings of your decisions. You are the one who must choose to receive or to decline the great offering. You are the one who must be responsible for everything that you do.

So do not go around telling people that God is guiding you to do this or that, for that is irresponsible. You must say, "I am doing this because I feel it is the thing that must be done." Claim no other authority, for you do not know for sure.

You cannot know the Assembly or the power of the presence that lives within you unless Knowledge has been activated within you and is beginning to emerge powerfully in your life. Do not create a romance about your angelic experience, whatever it may be, whether it be real or fabricated, because it is all about the emergence of Knowledge within you, you see.

The Assembly is only concerned with this, for until this happens, you are not reliable. You are not responsible. You are not courageous. You are not authentic. You are still subject to the persuasions of the world and to your own fears and preferences. You are too weak.

That is why you must be elevated within yourself through a process of great transformation that can only be initiated by the Assembly. You cannot initiate yourself. You can meditate for twenty years and not know of the power and the presence of Knowledge.

It is your prayer given now with the greatest strength, urgency and authenticity that calls the Assembly to you. You pray not for advantages or merely protection from harm. You pray to be redeemed, not knowing what this means, not trying to understand the redemption, not thinking you know how to purify yourself. For only the Assembly knows this.

It is a marvelous thing, you see. It is the greatest miracle of all. It is the miracle that creates every other miracle.

God has now sent a New Message into the world to prepare humanity to face a new world experience and environment, and to meet the great challenge of preserving and uniting human civilization.

God has sent the great Revelation into the world to prepare humanity for its encounter with life in the universe—the greatest event in human history and the one that poses the greatest challenges, difficulties and opportunities for the human family.

A Messenger is in the world. He has been in preparation for a very long time to receive the Revelation, for it is the largest Revelation ever given to humanity—given now to an educated world, a literate world, a world of global communication, a world of global awareness, to a certain degree.

It is the first time in history that a Message has been given to the whole world all at once. For it must reach the world in a short period of time to prepare humanity for the great change that is coming to the world and for the meaning of its encounter with intelligent life in the universe, which is occurring in the world already.

None of God's previous Revelations can prepare you for these things, for that was not their purpose or their design. They were given to build human awareness, human civilization and human conscience and the ethics that could possibly guide humanity to a greater unity and a greater power in the world.

Human civilization has been created, and though it is very imperfect—full of corruption and division and error—it nonetheless has great promise. If you knew the conditions of life in the universe around you, you would see this great promise. But you cannot see this yet. You do not have this vantage point. But the Assembly sees this, of course, and that is why great emphasis is being given to this world, to prepare for this great threshold. So much is being given now, through the process of Revelation.

But the Messenger faces great difficulties, the same difficulties all the previous Messengers faced—disbelief, antagonism, rejection, ridicule.

People cannot see that the greatest event in the world is occurring in their midst. They think it is a violation of their ideas, a challenge to their beliefs. They think it will undermine their wealth, their power and their prestige in the world when in fact it offers the greatest promise of redemption they could ever receive and the greatest preparation for a future that will be unlike the past in so many ways.

The Assembly watches and guides the Messenger, for his importance in the world cannot be underestimated. His importance in the world cannot be overestimated. The Assembly will speak through him to bring the Revelation into the world. And they will speak as one because the Message is everything.

If this can be recognized by enough people, heeded and followed by enough people, humanity will have the power to turn away from disintegration and endless conflict and war to build a new foundation for the future.

The Revelation has given the vision for this greater world for humanity, but it will be a very different world. It will require great power, courage and honesty to create it and to sustain it in a universe where there are powerful forces and where freedom is rare. Only God knows how this can be done. Only the Assembly understands these things.

Your task now is to learn to receive and to take the Steps to Knowledge so that you may find your true foundation in life, to challenge your ideas, to resolve dilemmas from the past, to forgive yourself and others, and to look upon the world without rejection and condemnation. For it is this world that will call forth from you, in time, your greater gifts and your greater role.

There is so much to unlearn here, so much to reconsider. You have to be humble enough to do this. If you think you know the truth, if you think you know God's Will, if you think you know what the universe is, your chances of discovering the truth will be very small.

The Assembly watches over the world. Call to the Assembly—not casually, for they will not hear you. Not to fulfill your ambitions, your dreams or your fantasies, for they will not hear you. You must pray with your heart and your soul. Only then can your voice reach them, for they only know what is true, honest and pure.

They cannot be manipulated. They cannot be corrupted. They cannot be influenced. You cannot make a deal with them. For you must have the strength to receive their counsel in time and carry it forth without compromise, without corruption. That is how strong you will have to be, to be part of a greater force for good in the world.

People will think, "Oh, this is too much for me to consider. The challenge is too great!" But We say no. It is appropriate for who you are and why you are in the world and who sent you here. You think of yourself in such a demeaning way. You have degraded to a pathetic state when you think like this. You do not know your strength, your power or your purpose, which only Knowledge within you can provide.

The Assembly watches and waits for those who can respond to the Message that God is sending into the world at this moment. For the Messenger is now coming forth to speak, to proclaim and to teach the Revelation. He has been withheld for a long time until the Message was complete. Now it is complete, and the world is in great need of it, greater than you can realize at this moment.

The Messenger represents the Assembly though he is a human being and though he is imperfect, for all human beings are imperfect. He has made mistakes, but all the great Messengers have made mistakes.

It is the Power of Heaven within him that is his strength, that is his banner, that is his shield. You can destroy his body, but you cannot destroy his Message. And you cannot destroy what he is bringing into the world and the Power and the Presence that has sent him here—the Power and the Presence that waits for you to respond.

For the gift is now before you, and Heaven watches and waits to see who can receive, who can recognize, who can take the Steps to Knowledge and receive the gift of a greater life in a world that grows darker and more uncertain with each passing day.

CHAPTER 11

GOD'S NEW MESSAGE
FOR THE WORLD

As revealed to
Marshall Vian Summers
on February 28, 2011
in Boulder, Colorado

It is time to receive a New Message from God. It is time to receive the gift, the power and the blessing. It is time to recognize that God has spoken again, after such a long silence.

For humanity is now facing the Great Waves of change—great environmental, economic and social change. It is facing its greatest challenges, its most difficult obstacles and its greatest call for unity and cooperation.

Receive then the New Message and take it to heart. Make it your study. Make it your emphasis. Do not condemn it or dispute it, or you will not be able to receive the power and the grace, the wisdom and the strength that it provides.

See the world now at a great turning point, where ever growing numbers of people will be drinking from a slowly shrinking well. Look out beyond the horizon and not merely into the near future, and you will see the Great Waves are building there. You will see that humanity will have to change and to adapt to a new set of circumstances and that nature, so long ignored and maligned, will now set the terms of engagement.

It is the time of great reckoning. It is a time of great accounting. It is not the end for humanity, but it is a great turning point. And it represents a new beginning—a new beginning that cannot be avoided or neglected.

The foolish will persist. The blind will continue to think that the future will be like the past. And those who are unaware will proclaim that they know what must be done for the world.

But despite the greatest and most accurate pronouncements and theories, you must have a New Revelation, or the obstacles will be too great and too formidable, the dangers too overwhelming, the human spirit too weak and too diffracted, the nations too divided and too self-serving and contentious.

It is a time when humanity will have to rethink its position in the world and to shift its priorities from growth and expansion to stability and security for the world's welfare and for the world's peoples.

It is the time that requires vision, a time that will challenge those who have built their careers on their theories and their systems of belief; a time when the welfare of your children and their children will have to be seriously considered instead of merely assumed; a time when the world's resources will have to be preserved rather than merely squandered and overused; a time when the needs of the poorer nations will be directly influencing the welfare of the stronger nations; a time to cease your endless conflicts to build an infrastructure that can sustain the human family.

Nations will have to cooperate, or they will become increasingly imperiled and endangered. Resources will become ever more expensive and difficult to acquire. Food production will be lost. The climates of the world are changing. Technology alone will not be able to meet many of the great challenges to come.

That is why there is a New Revelation, a New Message from God, because humanity cannot and has not responded sufficiently—except perhaps with a few exceptional individuals—to the specter of change that is upon you and before you.

It is not merely a question of adaptation. It is a question of fundamental change—a change of heart, a change of approach, a change of attitude. For what has worked before may not work now. What has been assumed may prove to be ineffectual and inadequate. Everything will have to be reconsidered.

The Revelation will reveal this and why it is true. It will speak to what those who can see have already experienced and are experiencing now. It will resonate with the great truths of all your religions, and yet it will reveal things that have never been revealed before. It is a Message to the individual who is struggling to see and know the truth. And it is a Message to the whole world, which is facing the Great Waves of change.

It is not a question of being positive or negative. It is a question of whether you can see or not, whether you have the eyes to see and the ears to hear. It is not a question of political orientation or ideology or school of thought. It is a question of whether you can see or respond—not only to the events of this day, but to the events to come, the events that are heading your way, the conditions of the world that are changing underneath your feet and that have changed the world already to such an extent that you are living and facing a different kind of world.

It is not the world of your parents or your ancestors. It is not the world upon which civilization has been built and made secure. It is not the world upon which human theory and philosophy have evolved over centuries of time. It is a different, more difficult and uncertain world—a world of deterioration, a world of change, a world that even science will not be able to comprehend fully, a world that is yours now.

You will need a greater intelligence to navigate this world. You will need the power of Knowledge within the individual to know and to see what must be done. You will need a great cooperation between the peoples and the nations, or the outcome will be catastrophic.

The New Message provides the key and missing elements. It will not address everything. It will not solve every problem. It will not answer every question. Of course not. But it will give you the priorities of your life and the priorities of the future. It will enable you to prepare for things you cannot see and do not yet know. It will give you the strength to reconsider your ideas and beliefs. It will restore to you the power of vision, and with it the eyes to see and the ears to hear.

Not everyone will receive this. Not everyone will respond. Not everyone will learn and bear witness to the New Message. Certainly not. But many will have to—in positions of leadership, in the population, in different countries, different cultures, different religions—because this is a Message for the world.

It is not a message for one country. It is not a Message for one time or one event. It is not a reaction to religion. It is not a rejection of religion. It is not a rejection of government. It is not a rejection of what exists, but a warning, a blessing and a preparation to live and to advance in a different world.

You cannot rely now upon what has occurred before. Even nature has been so disrupted that you will not be able to rely upon certain things.

Nations will struggle economically. There will be growth, but only temporarily. And the needs of the human family will so far exceed the capacity, or seemingly so, that it will overwhelm any progress that you can make.

This will create a change in priority. Security now will not merely be protecting one nation from another. It will be securing the stability of large populations of people. Everyone will have to be involved in this to some degree. It is not only a question for governments or governance. It is the whole world.

Many people will be lost in this great transition. But the losses can be minimized, and the tragedies can be mitigated. It will take everyone to participate for humanity to survive the Great Waves of change and to be in a position to build a new and more cooperative world—a world based not upon endless growth and expansion, but upon the stability and security of the peoples of the world. It will be a future very different from the past and very different from the world that you see at this moment.

Only God knows what is coming over the horizon. But you are given eyes to see and ears to hear so that you may see the evidence of this, today and tomorrow and in the days to follow. You are not asked to believe, but to pay attention, to clear your mind, to open your perception. The least sophisticated amongst you can tell that the winds are changing, while the experts keep debating realities from the past. It is not a question of intellectual brilliance. It is a question of attention and clarity, vision and discernment.

Many people will fail. Many people will deny. Many people will avoid reality, for this is one of the great weaknesses of humanity. Therefore, those who are strong, those who are clear, those who can see, those who are committed to serving a changing world will be ever more important in the future, in whatever position they assume in culture and society.

That is why the Revelation must be given. It is not a human invention. It is not the product of one man's thinking or imagination. Hardly so. It is not a revolution against religious thinking as it exists today. It is entirely new. It does not come to condemn, but to correct and to give you the power to create. It is a Message for the world.

The darkening skies are growing. The difficulties of humanity are escalating. Governments will become impotent in the face of this unless guided by a greater vision and a greater commitment.

Humanity is still emerging from a primitive state, a tribal state, into a world community. It is a very difficult and dangerous transition, but it must occur, as it must occur in all worlds in the universe where intelligent life has evolved.

You are now facing these great and difficult transitions, from tribal warlike societies to a world community—a community based upon necessity and not merely ideology, a community based upon securing and protecting the world from internal collapse and protecting it from foreign intervention from the universe around you.

It is a different world than the world you think of today, but it is a world in keeping with nature, for nature has not changed. The world has changed, but humanity has not changed with it. And now you are entering new territory. Foreign and dangerous it is. It will require great care as you proceed into the future.

What will guide human perception? What will inform people's decisions? That is why there is a New Revelation, brought into the world by one man with a small group of assistants. He is the

Messenger for this time, but he will not fit the expectations of a superman. He will not have magical powers. He will not be charismatic. He will not be entertaining. But he is the Messenger, and it is his life that has been the vehicle for the transmission of a New Message from God.

Receive then. Listen. Open your minds. You cannot navigate the future without this greater Revelation. You will not be prepared. You will not prepare in time. You will not be able to convince others to respond.

God loves the world and has given humanity great Teachings at important turning points to establish human civilization and to free people from tribal identity, to enable civilization to evolve and to grow despite its many tragedies and errors.

Now you are moving from a civilization to a world community, for only this will provide [real security] and protect the human family into the future. It is a transition that few can even think of constructively at this moment. But it is your destiny.

CHAPTER 12

GOD IS MOVING HUMANITY IN A NEW DIRECTION

As revealed to
Marshall Vian Summers
on April 22, 2011
in Boulder, Colorado

God is moving humanity in a new direction, a direction it has not had to move in before. For the world has changed, and humanity is facing a Greater Community of life in the universe—a great change, a great threshold in humanity's long evolution, a time of immense upheaval and uncertainty, a dangerous time for the human family, a time that will be moving with events unfolding quickly.

God is moving humanity in a new direction, towards a world community that is able to sustain the world, that is able to encounter the realities of life in the universe, which will be thrust upon you and are being thrust upon you even at this moment. It is a great change that many people feel, but do not comprehend.

The movement of the world is accelerating, where people's lives will be overwhelmed and overtaken by the great environmental change that is taking place and through political and economic upheaval. All of this is now in motion and cannot be stopped, only mitigated. This will require a great adaptation.

It is at this great threshold in humanity's history that a New Revelation has been sent into the world, and a Messenger has been sent here to receive it, to prepare it and to present it. For him, it is a long journey, a long and difficult journey.

The Message for humanity now is great, more comprehensive and complete than any Message that has ever been sent into the world, complete with teaching and commentary so that its wisdom and Knowledge can be discerned and applied correctly and not simply left up to human interpretation.

People do not see, do not hear. They are strangers to themselves. And their native skills of discerning the environment, for many, have been lost and are undeveloped.

This makes the Messenger's task more difficult. He must carry the Mystery, for the Revelation is beyond the realm of the intellect and certainly is not conditioned by people's expectations, beliefs or comprehension.

God is moving the world in a new direction. It is a direction that was always intended, but it will be new for the people of the world. It will be new to your understanding.

The great Revelations from the Creator are always like this. They are always presenting a new reality, a new awareness, a new dimension and a greater promise.

The world is growing dark, and this greater promise is needed now. Only the light of Knowledge, the greater intelligence that the Creator has bestowed upon the human family and upon all the races in the universe, only this now can enable you to comprehend and respond.

For you return to God on God's terms. And God's Messages must be comprehended, as they truly are and are intended to be.

There will be much struggle and contention with this, and the Messenger and the Messenger's followers must face this difficulty, this frustration, and exercise great patience.

Such a Revelation will not be accepted at the outset, and only the few will be able to respond completely. But as time moves forward and as the world grows more turbulent, the New Message will gain a greater attraction, greater recognition and greater relevance.

It is answering questions you have not even asked. It is a preparation for the future as well as a remedy for the present.

Your philosophers and theologians will not know what to make of it. They will have issues with it. It will not conform to their understanding, to which they have invested themselves so greatly. Religious leaders will contend against it because it speaks of a reality that they do not yet recognize.

God is moving humanity in a new direction. The Messenger is here to provide the Revelation. It has taken him decades to receive it. It will take decades for it to be recognized in the world.

But the problem is time. Humanity does not have much time to prepare for a new world and for contact with life in the universe—contact which is occurring already, contact with a dangerous purpose and intention.

People are obsessed with their needs, their issues, their longing and their desires. They do not see the movement of the world. For the world has changed, but people have not changed with it. And now you are facing a new set of realities.

What will God say to this as people feel overwhelmed, as their prophecies for the future do not come true, as the return of their savior does not occur, as they believe that God is creating all these problems for them?

The Revelation speaks to all these things. But you must be open to the Revelation, and you must face the prospect of great change, for it is upon you and the world, and it is going to move forward.

You cannot go backwards thousands of years and try to comprehend what is occurring today. For humanity's evolution has moved into a new position, a position of dominance in the world and a position of greater vulnerability in the universe.

Where will this education begin to prepare you for a new world and for the Greater Community of life—two events that will alter the course of human history and affect the life of every person?

The governments do not know. The religious leaders do not know. The experts do not know. The universities cannot prepare people.

The Revelation must come from the Creator of all life, and this is what is occurring now. For you are living in a time of Revelation, and the Messenger is in the world. As long as he is in the world, you have an opportunity to receive and to prepare. When he is gone, it will be different. It will be more difficult. In this, he is the Light in the world.

He is a humble man and makes no claims other than to be the Messenger, for that is the role that has been assigned to him. He must prepare humanity for a new world through the Revelation. He must prepare humanity for the Greater Community through the Revelation. He must speak of the great change that is coming and that is already upon the people everywhere, through the Revelation.

God is moving humanity in a new direction. Can humanity move? Can people respond? Can you respond? Can you accept that you are living in a time of Revelation and to consider what this means for your life and the challenge this places before you?

People do not realize how much their life and circumstances are dependent upon the condition of the world and the movement of the world. Only in the poorer nations is this greater reality ever present. In affluent nations, the affluence insulates you from the greater realities of life to a certain extent for a period of time. But this affluence will diminish, and the greater realities are upon you.

How humanity responds and prepares will make all the difference. What informs individuals' decisions will make all the difference. What voice they listen to, whether it be the power and the presence of Knowledge that God has given to them to guide them and to protect them, or whether it be the voice of their culture or the voice of fear or the voice of anger or ambition.

These choices are fundamental for the individual, and what individuals decide will determine the fate and the future of humanity. Therefore, the responsibility falls upon everyone, not only on leaders and institutions.

That is why God is bringing the New Message to the people and not to the leaders of nations. For the leaders are not free. They are bound by their office and to those who got them elected, to the expectations of others. That is why the Revelation is coming to you and to the people. It is their decisions and determination that will make all the difference.

People want many things. They do not want to lose what they have. They are caught up in the moment. They do not have the perspective to see where their life is going.

The Revelation will be a great shock and a great challenge to each person. But this shock and challenge is the shock of Revelation. The challenge is being confronted with the Will of the Creator. The challenge is whether you can respond and the nature of your response.

You cannot stand where you are, for the world has changed, and it will change further. It is moving. You must move with it. This is being in harmony with life. This is coming out of isolation. This is freeing yourself from distraction and obsession. This is learning to listen, to look, to still your mind so that you may see. This is giving up grievances so that you may understand where you are. This is taking the Steps to Knowledge so that the Presence and the Power of God may speak through you and to you.

This is the Revelation taking humanity in a new direction. Are people willing to go, or will they stay behind—facing the Great Waves of change, asleep on the beach as the Great Waves build, living on the shoreline thinking that all is well, living for the moment, unable to respond to the signs of the world, living under assumptions that are not in keeping with the realities of life?

Who can respond? Who will look? Who will listen? Who will set aside their ideas, their beliefs and their preferences long enough to see something, to hear something, to know something?

This is what the Messenger will ask you to do. This is what the Revelation requires. This is what living in a new world requires. This is what emerging into a Greater Community of life requires.

Will humanity be foolish and clumsy, ignorant and unresponsive, its greater intelligence not being recognized and utilized? These are the questions. The answers are not apparent, for they have not yet come into being. They have not met the real test that is upon the human family.

But the Creator of all life loves the world and loves humanity and has sent the power of redemption into the world—to redeem the individual and to restore their power and integrity, to meet the great challenges of life that are now emerging on the horizon.

God is moving humanity in a new direction. It is time to prepare, to receive and to support the Revelation.

People will complain. They will protest. They will resist. They will accuse the Messenger. They will denounce the Revelation. Unable to respond, unwilling to reconsider their life and their ideas, they will resist.

This always happens at the time of Revelation. Those who have the greatest investment in the past will resist the new world and everything in it. They cannot see. They will not know. They do not have the courage to reconsider their position. They do not have the humility to stand in the face of the Revelation.

What can God do for them? They asked so much from the Creator, but they cannot respond to the Creator's response. What can God do for them?

Be amongst the first to respond so that your greater gifts in life may be established and have an opportunity to come forth in the days and the years of your life.

This is the power of Revelation—to unleash wisdom and Knowledge that humanity desperately needs now to prepare for a future that will be unlike the past.

The blessings are with you. The power of redemption is within you, in Knowledge within you. But what can ignite this Knowledge and call it forth and enable you to approach it, to understand it and to follow it successfully?

It must be ignited by God. The Revelation is here to set in motion the greater redemption of individuals in preparation for the new world and for humanity's destiny in the universe, which are yet to be recognized and fulfilled.

It is time to respond. It is time to be really honest with yourself, not basing your life on your preferences or your fears, but on true recognition within yourself.

Facing the Revelation will challenge you to respond with this deeper honesty. Facing the Revelation will challenge you with this deeper honesty. It is the greatest challenge of your life. It is the most important challenge of your life. It is the most important event of your life.

God is moving humanity in a new direction.

CHAPTER 13

THE WORLD MUST RECEIVE GOD'S NEW MESSAGE

As revealed to
Marshall Vian Summers
on January 1, 2015
in Alexandria, Egypt

God knows what is coming for the world. God knows the condition of the world and its people. And the Angelic Presence that oversees this world is watching every moment.

It is no secret to those who watch over you what your greater needs are, both in this moment and in the times to come.

You cannot see these things, for you do not know yourself fully. You do not know why you were sent into the world, or where you should be at this moment and why you are not there at this moment. You cannot see what is coming over the distant horizon, coming your way. But those who watch over you and the Lord of the universe know these things.

People are bound by their beliefs and their assumptions. They are bound by the interpretation of religions from the past, which makes it even more difficult for them to understand that God has spoken again for the protection and advancement of humanity.

Everything God has ever given to the world in the great Messages, given at times of great need and opportunity, has been given for the advancement and the protection of humanity.

You do not realize you are living in a world within a Greater Community of life, where there are many threats to human freedom and sovereignty. You do not see the big picture of your life or why you were sent into the world at this time, to serve the world under these circumstances. But Heaven can see these things, which you, living in your state of Separation, cannot see.

You are further blinded by your assumptions and beliefs, your attitudes and your condemnation of others.

People live for the moment. They have forgotten they must also prepare for the future. Like all intelligent creatures on Earth, they must do these two things.

But God knows what is coming. God knows what humanity needs at this time. God knows what you, as an individual, must have to recognize your greater purpose for coming and why you were sent and what you must accomplish here, which is beyond your understanding.

For your intellect is not big enough to hold greater things of this nature. It is a perfect mechanism for navigating the world of changing circumstances, but it cannot understand your life beyond time and space, and the greater forces that direct you and have sent you here and who hold for you your greater purpose in being here.

Now God has spoken again, giving a Revelation greater and more vast than anything that has ever been given to the human family before, given now to a literate world of global communication and growing global awareness, given now at a time when the world is entering a state of decline—declining resources, a declining environment, a changing atmosphere, all wrought by human ignorance, greed and corruption.

So humanity stands blindly at the threshold of precipitous change that could alter the face of the world, the greatest change that has ever come for the human family as a whole.

But people are living in the moment and do not see the signs of the world. They do not hear the signs within themselves—warning them, alerting them, telling them to hold back, telling them to reconsider so that they may have a moment of seeing, a moment of clarity, so that they may have a moment to hear the greater voice that God has put within them, the voice of Knowledge.

Deep beneath the surface of the mind it is. It is trying to take you somewhere, to prepare you for a greater service in the world and to prepare you for a world of monumental change and upheaval.

God has spoken now to the whole world, not to one little group, not to one region alone, not to one religious tradition, not to one educated class of people, but to everyone at all stations of society, in all societies.

For the world must hear God's New Revelation, or it will not prepare for the great future, for the new world it is just beginning to experience. It will not end its ceaseless conflicts but degrade the world even further, casting humanity into ever greater darkness and confusion.

The world must hear God's New Revelation. For the great traditions of the past were not meant to prepare humanity for this great threshold in your evolution. They cannot prepare you for a universe full of intelligent life. They cannot prepare you for a world in decline, a world that will alter everything that you see and know.

They were given at different times in history to build human civilization, to build and reinforce true humanitarianism, true human ethics and high principles. Though many have not been able to follow these things, they had to be established or humanity would be forever a primitive, violent, self-destructive race, degrading a beautiful world, which is so rare in a universe of barren planets and inhospitable places.

The world must hear of God's New Revelation because it alone holds the key to your future, to your safety, to human unity, purpose and cooperation. There are too few people in the world who value these sufficiently to be able to change and alter the course that you are plotting for yourself, even at this moment. It must come from God— your Source, the Creator of all life, the Creator of everything.

But for this, you must hear with new ears. You must listen with an open heart. If you reject this, then you reject the God that you claim to praise and believe in. You reject the awareness that God's Plan is greater than just one Revelation at one given time in history.

For all the Messengers have come from the Angelic Assembly, and they are all serving in a Greater Plan for humanity—to build human civilization, to further human unity and cooperation, to teach humanity, through wisdom and through its technology, how to sustain a beautiful world and not plunder it into a state of total decay.

It is a Greater Plan. Even from the beginning, it was to prepare you for your future in a Greater Community of life in the universe. But first it [humanity] must become a viable civilization. It must have higher ethics and principles to be a free world and to have any freedom in a universe where freedom is so very rare.

The Plan was always there. It has not changed, but only adapted itself to changing circumstances and to shifting moments of great opportunity.

You cannot see this, you who live in the moment, you who are circumscribed by a world you do not understand, you who live in your thoughts and beliefs and admonitions, but cannot feel yet the greater Presence that abides with you and that is your Source, your purpose and your destiny.

It is necessary that the world hear God's New Revelation. For only God knows what is coming. Only God knows how you can prepare. Only God understands you better than you understand yourself. Only God knows the true condition of humanity and what humanity must do to save itself from collapse from within and from the risk of subjugation by others from without.

Do not stand behind your scriptures and deny this, for this is the further work of God in the world. This fulfills the work of Muhammad and the Jesus and the Buddha and the other great teachers—known and unknown, recognized and unrecognized—in the history of this world, whom you cannot even account for completely.

Do not be arrogant and foolish, or you will fail in the face of the Great Waves of change that are coming. And you will not prepare for your encounter with a universe of intelligent life, an encounter that is already taking place by forces who are here to take advantage of a weak and unsuspecting humanity.

The risks are growing each day. The Greater Darkness is in the world.

Humanity is destroying its foundation in this world with unprecedented haste and foolishness—unable to restrain itself, unable to change course, unable to provide for the greater needs of people everywhere, unable or unwilling to do what must be done to secure humanity's future under a different set of circumstances.

You cannot prepare yourself. You do not yet have the courage. You do not yet see the need. You do not yet recognize the signs. You do not yet have the cooperation amongst you, between you, between your nations, between your religions, who are now descending into ever growing chaos and dissension between one another and even within themselves.

It is not that you are helpless. It is just that you are irresponsible. It is not that you do not have certain strengths and abilities. It is that you are lost in a world of fear and desire, conflict, poverty and deprivation—a world you have created.

You cannot blame God for this. You cannot even blame God for the natural catastrophes—the droughts, the hurricanes, the pestilence— because this is all part of nature functioning, which was set in motion at the beginning of time.

So the Angelic Assembly watches over you and all others here to see how you will adapt, to see what you will choose. They have given you freedom to live in Separation. They have given you the freedom even to fail. But they have also given you the power and direction to succeed—if you can respond, if you can respond to this greater guidance, if you can respond to Knowledge within yourself, which is still connected to God.

The Lord of this universe and other universes and of Creation, the timeless Creation beyond all physical manifestation, is not attending to you physically or personally. That is for the Assembly to do. For there are countless races in the universe, and each must have an Assembly to oversee them.

It is a Plan on a scale that you cannot possibly even consider. So great, so vast, so encompassing, so perfect, only God could do it. Only God can reclaim the separated through the power of Knowledge that has been placed within all sentient life.

You have now an opportunity to understand these things in a Revelation far more advanced and complete. For you do not yet understand how God works in the world, working through people from the inside out—through service, through contribution, through forgiveness and through constructive and compassionate behavior.

Your notions of God are born of Teachings from antiquity. They are incomplete, for people at that time did not have the sophistication or the freedom or the social development to understand the greater nature of God's Plan in this world and beyond.

The great religions have kept humanity going, have built human civilization, have been an inspiration for countless people. Do not think they are without value, despite all that has been done in violation of them, and how they have been misused and are being misused even at this day.

God has put Knowledge within you, a perfect guiding intelligence. It is connected to God. It is not afraid of the world. It is not conditioned by the world. It is not drawn by beauty, wealth and charm. It is only here to take you to a rendezvous with your greater mission in life and a reunion with those who sent you—a life of purpose, meaning, relationship and inspiration.

But you are far adrift. If you are to be amongst the first to respond, you must respond strongly. Do not linger in doubt, for that is dishonest. In your heart you will know, you will understand what We are saying here today. It is a challenge. It is a challenge to be honest, to be sincere and to be wholehearted.

The world must hear God's New Revelation. It is not for you alone. It is not for your edification alone. But you are meant to be a part of it, to receive it, to express it, to share it and to help translate it into every language of the world so that enough people in the world might respond and begin to change the course of humanity, to evoke the kind of responsibilities and change that must occur for the human family to not fall into grave instability, conflict and war.

You do not yet see the risks facing you now. So it is hard for you to understand the great need that has brought this to the world.

For this, you must open your eyes to the world, not to what you want, not to what you prefer, but to what is really happening here. You must become a responsible person—a person able to respond.

For you must hear God's New Revelation, and you must bring to it as much honesty and sincerity and humility as you can. It will strengthen you in all ways. It will bring resolution to your life. It will restore you from shame and unworthiness. It will bring you back to yourself and to the true direction that you must follow, which God has already placed within you to receive now.

The Messenger is in the world. He is the one who was sent to bring this here. He is a humble man. He has no worldly position. He does not seek to lead nations or armies or one group against another, for he has a Message for the whole world—to either receive or to reject.

Time is of the essence now. The Great Waves of change are beginning to strike everywhere, here and there, each year degrading your infrastructure, your societies, your wealth and your self-confidence. It is the time to prepare, but the time is not long. It is short. It is now.

But not everyone can respond. For not everyone will know of it. Not everyone is even ready for it. And many will stand against it, protecting their former ideas and beliefs, their wealth or their position in society. It is unfortunate, but it always happens at the time of Revelation.

Let you be amongst the first to receive God's New Revelation for the world. It is of the greatest value. It is the most important thing in your life. It will make all the difference after everything else has failed you. It will make all the difference for you if you can receive it and follow it and take the Steps to Knowledge that God has provided to re-engage you with your deeper purpose and nature in being here.

If humanity should fail to receive the great Revelation, then it will enter into a state of permanent decline—great conflict, great human suffering and loss. For you will not be prepared for this new world. You will not be prepared for what is coming even though the signs appear every day.

You will try to protect your interests, your preferences, your hopes. You do not want to really have to deal with the things that are coming your way. But to deal with them will give you strength and courage and determination. Without this preparation, you will not have these strengths and capabilities.

It is a great Revelation for you. It is a great Revelation for humanity. For it will honor all the world's religions and unite them sufficiently that they will cease their endless conflicts. You will see that they are all connected at their foundation, regardless of what has been made out of them over time.

You will see that all the Messengers have come from the Assembly. And you will see that no one else can claim to bring great Revelations into the world if they do not have this Source. For though there are prophets in every age, the great Messages only come at great turning points. And they bring with them a whole new reality that could alter the course of the world and the destiny of countless people who can respond over time.

There is a great need for the world to receive God's New Revelation. This is your challenge. This is your redemption. There is nothing more important for you to consider now.

The Messenger is an older man. He will only be in the world for a few more years, perhaps. If you can meet him and know of him, it will be a great blessing for you.

He is not a god, but none of the Messengers were gods. He will not allow you to praise him, for all praise must go to God and to the Assembly. He has proven himself through suffering and isolation, through great challenges and great preparation, beyond the understanding of people around him, save but a few.

We bring this to you because it is the Will of Heaven. It is We who spoke to the Jesus, the Buddha and the Muhammad. It is We who watch over the world. You cannot know Our names. Our names are not important, for We speak as one and many, and many as one—a reality that you cannot embrace, living in Separation, not yet.

The Will of Heaven is that humanity will prepare for the Greater Community, it will become strong and united, and it will preserve this world so it will not fall under the persuasion and domination of other nations who seek to use this world for their own purposes.

For the first time in history, the doors of the universe are being thrown open for you to see what life is like in the universe around you and what God is doing in this universe. For to understand what God is doing in this world, you must understand what God is doing in the universe—essentially, fundamentally—and this is being made available for the very first time.

May your eyes be open. May your understanding of the world be true and honest. May your evaluation of yourself and your needs be sincere and filled with humility and earnestness. And may the Gift of Heaven that you are receiving now—so fortunate you are to be living at a time of Revelation—be yours to recognize, to receive and to give to a world in great need.

CHAPTER 14

THE CALLING

As revealed to
Marshall Vian Summers
on April 1, 2011
in Boulder, Colorado

To live in a time of Revelation and to be presented with this Revelation is a monumental event. So great it will be that it will change your life and your thinking, your perception and your understanding of yourself, the world and your destiny. Even if you refuse the New Message and dispute it, it will still change your life.

You cannot come upon something this great and not have it impact your life. You cannot come upon a Revelation, the likes of which are only given centuries apart, without having it have a great impact upon you.

No matter how you might respond in the moment, it will reach deeper within you, to a place you may hardly know, to a part of yourself you have only experienced in moments of clarity and great sobriety. It will speak down through the Ancient Corridors of your mind.

Should you study it and read it and follow its direction, you will begin to hear things and see things that you did not hear and see before. You will have a greater vision and a more encompassing understanding, an understanding that is not merely self-serving and self-gratifying, but something that can face reality and that can appreciate your being in the world at this time.

If this were not a New Message from God, you could treat it at the level of ideas alone. You could treat it as a theory. You could treat it as a philosophy. You could treat it as just another teaching. But it is far greater than this.

That is why if you respond at all, it will have an impact upon your life. It is meant to have an impact on your life.

You are called to receive it, to study it and to learn of it. Only here will you realize its validity and its great relevance to the world you see today and to the world you will have to face in the future times—the great change that is coming over the horizon and all that humanity will have to face, the great trials and the great opportunities that await you.

It is a great thing to come upon God's Revelation—greater than your ideas, greater than your beliefs, greater than your institutions, greater even than the ideas and beliefs of your nation or culture or religion. For these are human inventions, mostly.

But now you are encountering something that is not a product of human imagination or creativity. You will know this to be true because of the impact it will have.

It comes from your Source—the greatest love of your life, the Source of your life, the Source of your deeper nature, the Source of your purpose for being in the world, which still remains unknown to you and unfulfilled.

This is the answer to the great prayers uttered in recent times and throughout history for peace, for deliverance, for wisdom and for strength.

You cannot give this greater power to yourself, though many have tried. It must be bestowed upon you from a greater Source—a Source that defies definition, a Source that cannot be conceptualized or comprehended with the intellect.

For the Creator lives beyond the realm of the intellect, and the Creation with it. You can only comprehend your immediate circumstances and the sequence of events, but beyond this is a Greater Reality, far greater indeed.

The New Message requires things of you. It requires you to respond. It requires you to study and to be patient and not to come to premature conclusions, not to follow your prejudices, your anger or your resentments. It asks you to explore, not just to believe, for belief is weak. It is not substantial enough.

You will need a greater foundation within yourself to face a changing world and to face all that humanity must face in this time of Revelation.

This is not merely a gift to you personally. It is meant to flow through you to others. If you are to receive, then you must give. You must bear witness to the Revelation.

You must honor the Messenger. He is not a god and will not allow people to worship him. But he is the Messenger, and there is no one else in the world who has brought a New Message from God here.

It has been a long time since a Revelation has been given of this magnitude. And never before has a Revelation been given so completely, given now to a literate world—a world of planetary communication, a world of greater sophistication, a world of greater need.

You do not realize it yet, but it is destiny that you should find this. It is no mere accident or happenstance. It is destiny that you should encounter the New Revelation. It is destiny that you should hear of it.

It is a great calling. But what God wills and what people will do are not the same.

You are free to respond in any number of ways even though this is a gift to you, even though this holds the promise of revealing to you your greater purpose and destiny in the world and a greater comprehension of your life and the changing circumstances around you.

God cannot control your response. God cannot control your thoughts, your suffering, your confusion, your admonitions, your fervent beliefs, your complaints, your self-destructive behaviors, your poor mistakes and decisions.

That is because you are living in Separation. But there is a part of you that never separated from God, and this is what the New Message will speak to within you, a part of you that can only respond. It is the most natural thing in the world. It is your purpose and your destiny.

Should you receive it [the New Message], then you must share it with others. And you must bring it into your life and apply it there to the best of your ability and seek out others who are doing the same so that they may assist you in becoming strong and bringing balance and purpose to your affairs.

You cannot dispute a New Message from God. You will only appear to be foolish to the Greater Powers should you do this.

You will have many questions that you cannot answer and many questions that cannot be answered for some time indeed.

You must realize that this is a greater engagement. It is not an intellectual pursuit. It is not a pastime or a hobby. It is not here to give you pleasure, comfort and security. It is here to call you into a greater service in a world whose needs are escalating with each passing day.

Your obligation is because you have a greater purpose for being here—a purpose you did not invent and cannot invent, a purpose that has yet not been fully revealed to you, a purpose that is different from your wishes and your preferences and your ideas about your life.

You are obligated because you were sent into the world. The obligation lives within you. It is part of your deeper nature, a deeper nature We call Knowledge.

It [the obligation] is the pinnacle of all spiritual study, in all religions. It is what will redeem you. It is what will transform your life, your perception and your understanding. But it must be activated by God.

You have a responsibility to be in the world. You are accountable to those who sent you here. You have a greater role to play. You have a greater service to provide.

The New Message reminds you of your greater purpose, your responsibilities and your accountability. It does this without the threat of punishment or guilt. It does this to restore you, to save you from your own regret and suffering, to empower you to redeem your life and to bring balance there, for you have greater work to do in the world.

Only a New Revelation can have such a calling. It is a calling across the world. It is not just to one group or one nation, one religion or one part of society. It is now beginning to sound around the world.

It is a humble beginning. The New Message comes here like a seedling, like a child—pure, uncorrupted by the world, fragile, delicate, but with the Power of Creation behind it. As long as it can remain pure and the Messenger not be defiled, then its purity will ring forth.

You have this great opportunity to receive a pure Message, a Revelation for this time and the times to come.

Do you think this is an accident? Do you think this happens by chance? If so, you are underestimating what you are receiving here. And you are overestimating your own ideas and understanding.

God seeks to restore power to the individual so that those who were sent into the world may contribute to a world in need. The future of the world depends upon this.

Your role will be humble. It will not garner great attention and accolades. You will work behind the scenes, without fanfare and recognition. And in so doing, you will escape the prison house of your own mind and all that drives you and curses you and holds you back.

The New Message will be denied and disputed. It will be ridiculed. This always happens at a time of Revelation.

The Messenger will not meet people's expectations, for he is a simple and humble man. He is not godlike and all powerful and full of charm and charisma. No one with those qualities would ever be chosen to be a Messenger, to bring a New Message from God into the world.

He is without ambition. He has been in preparation for a very long time. It has taken him a very long time to receive the Message, for it is very great and comprehensive.

It will take you time to receive the New Message, for it is greater than what you think and believe and understand at this moment. It holds a window into a greater life in the world and to humanity's future and destiny within a Greater Community of life in the universe.

Nothing like this has ever been given to humanity before, but now it must be given. Now it is crucial in determining the future and the outcome that humanity will have to face.

Therefore, approach this with humility. Begin to consider that you too have a greater life and that you are not living this life yet, that you need great assistance and a great Revelation to understand and to take the journey to that greater life, to take the Steps to Knowledge, to be guided by a greater strength, a greater courage and a greater determination.

You were obligated before you even came into the world. That obligation lives within you now.

God's Revelations have the power to spark, to ignite and to initiate this deeper responsibility. Do not shrink from this, for all that is great and meaningful will come from this. All that is powerful, all that is compassionate, all that is freeing, all that is liberating will come from this.

God has planted the seeds of redemption within you, but they must be cultivated, and you must have the right approach and attitude. And the Calling must be there.

This is the obligation. It is only asking you to be honest, really honest, so honest that you can feel what you know, beyond your wishes, your fears and preferences, [so that] you can see the truth beyond what you want and what you deny.

The New Message asks you to be honest. How you respond will determine whether you are being honest and sincere.

It is not a matter of what you believe in, whether this fits with that. Why would God's Revelation ever fit with what you think or believe? It does not conform to human expectations, human conventions, long-established beliefs or human speculation because it is a New Message from God and not a product of human ideas.

It is preparing you for a non-human universe. You have no idea how to prepare yourself for that. It is preparing you for a world of diminishing resources and greater upheaval and tension. You have no idea how to prepare for that. It is preparing you to live a greater life. You have no idea how to achieve that.

God knows this, of course, and that is why the great Revelation must now be given, for this time and the times to come, calling upon the obligation that lives within people—for those who are ready to respond, for those who have the resident honesty and freedom to respond, for those who are not bound by their religious ideology, their cultural thinking or the will and preference of others.

This is the challenge of living in a time of Revelation. It will confront you with yourself—your strength and your weakness and the strength and weakness of those around you. It is a confrontation with a greater truth and a greater purpose.

Be grateful that this could be given to you. For without this, you would grope blindly in the world, chasing dreams and pleasures, always living under the threat of fear, the threat of deprivation, the weight of your own mind, a mind that is not being guided by Knowledge.

Be grateful, for the Lord of all the universes is giving to humanity exactly what it needs—not to answer all of its questions or to fulfill its aims and desires, but to give it exactly what it needs to find its strength and to proceed with a greater cooperation and harmony in the world.

You have come into the world at this time to serve under these circumstances. This is your time, a time of Revelation. This is your moment, a moment to exercise a deeper honesty and a deeper sincerity.

This is a calling—calling beyond your thinking and ideas, your feelings and emotions, to a deeper reality within you.

Do not try to understand this. It is beyond your understanding. Do not compare this with other things, for you do not know what you are looking at. You have not explored, lived and applied the New Message, so you cannot judge it with any wisdom or honesty or sincerity.

This is a gift to the world, but it must be given from person to person. You must bear witness to this to others, finding those who are ready and willing to respond. That is part of your purpose, you see. That is part of your gift. That is part of what awaits your deeper recognition.

You were meant to live in a time of Revelation. The Revelation is here. Your destiny is calling you. It is just a question of whether you are ready or not. You can only account for yourself in this regard.

You cannot determine what other people will say or do. It is a challenge to you and to each individual who has the blessing and the opportunity to receive a New Revelation from God. Do not worry what the others will do, what the world will do. This is a calling for you.

Only God knows how to reach the deeper part of you. You cannot find this on your own. Only God knows how to call forth that which is your greatest gift and service. You cannot call this out of yourself.

Only a New Revelation will prepare humanity for a future that will be unlike the past and for facing a greater reality of life in the universe.

Be grateful. Be humble. Be receptive. You do not need to believe, only to witness and to receive, to learn and to apply. The gifts will become apparent to you, and they will demonstrate their relevance and their perfection to you over time.

Humanity cannot fulfill itself. It must have great assistance. It cannot prepare itself for the future. It is too blind and arrogant at this moment. It does not see what is coming over the horizon, for it thinks it is still living in the past.

It does not see it is emerging into a Greater Community of life in the universe, a Greater Community that is challenging and difficult, where freedom is rare and where competition is extensive and carried on with great skill and persuasion.

Only God can prepare you for this. Only God knows the human heart and the human mind, the human soul and the human history.

You must accept your limitations in order to receive a greater comprehension. That is part of your calling.

Humanity, hear My words. We speak of a greater reality—a greater truth that lives within each person, a greater truth that cannot be comprehended by intellectual debate or speculation, a deeper truth that must be lived and experienced to be realized and to be expressed clearly.

Hear My words, people of this world. You have a greater destiny in the universe, but you must face a declining world. You must face the great upheavals that will come. You must unite together and cooperate with a greater clarity and determination.

This is the Revelation of God. It is a Revelation beyond human understanding. You can only approach it and begin to learn it, but you will never exhaust its wisdom, its clarity or its power.

IMPORTANT TERMS

*T*he New Message from God reveals that our world stands at the greatest threshold in the history and evolution of humanity. At this threshold, a New Message from God has come. It reveals the great change that is coming to the world and our destiny within the Greater Community of life beyond our world for which we are unaware and unprepared.

Here the Revelation redefines certain familiar terms but within a greater context and introduces other terms which are new to the human family. It is important to understand these terms when reading the texts of the New Message.

GOD is revealed in the New Message as the Source and Creator of all life and of countless races in the universe. Here the greater reality of God is unveiled in the expanded context of all life in this world and all life in the universe. This greater context redefines the meaning of our understanding of God and of God's Power and Presence in our lives. The New Message states that to understand what God is doing in our world, we must understand what God is doing in the entire universe. This is now being revealed for the first time through a New Message from God. In the New Message, God is not a personage or a singular awareness, but instead a pervasive force and reality that permeates all life, existing beyond the limited boundaries of all theology and religious understanding. God speaks to the deepest part of each person through the power of Knowledge that lives within them.

THE SEPARATION is the ongoing state and condition of being apart from God. The Separation began when part of Creation willed to have the freedom to be apart from God, to live in a state of Separation. As a result, God created our evolving world and the expanding universe as a place for the separated to live in countless forms and places. Before the Separation, all life was in a timeless state of pure union. It is to this original state of union with God that all those living in Separation are ultimately called to return—through service, contribution and the discovery of Knowledge. It is God's mission in our world and throughout the universe to reclaim the separated through Knowledge, which is the part of each individual still connected to God.

KNOWLEDGE is the deeper spiritual mind and intelligence within each person, waiting to be discovered. Knowledge represents the eternal part of us that has never left God. The New Message speaks of Knowledge as the great hope for humanity, an inner power at the heart of each person that God's New Message is here to reveal and to call forth. Knowledge exists beyond the intellect. It alone has the power to guide each of us to our higher purpose and destined relationships in life.

THE ANGELIC ASSEMBLY is the great Angelic Presence that watches over the world. This is part of the hierarchy of service and relationship established by God to oversee the redemption and return of all separate life in the universe. Every world where sentient life exists is watched over by an Angelic Assembly. The Assembly overseeing our world has translated the Will of God for our time into human language and understanding, which is now revealed through the New Message from God. The term Angelic Assembly is synonymous with the terms Angelic Presence and Angelic Host.

THE NEW MESSAGE FROM GOD is an original Revelation and communication from God to the people of the world, both for our time and the times to come. The New Message is a gift from the Creator of all life to people of all nations and religions, and represents the next great expression of God's Will and Plan for the human family. The New Message is over 9000 pages in length and is the largest Revelation ever given to the world, given now to a literate world of global communication and growing global awareness. The New Message is not an offshoot or reformation of any past tradition. It is a New Message from God for humanity which now faces great instability and upheaval in the world and the great threshold of emerging into a Greater Community of intelligent life in the universe.

THE VOICE OF REVELATION is the united voice of the Angelic Assembly, delivering God's Message through a Messenger sent into the world for this task. Here, the Assembly speaks as one Voice, the many speaking as one. For the very first time in history, you are able to hear the actual Voice of Revelation speaking through God's Messenger. It is this Voice that has spoken to all God's Messengers in the past. The Word and the Sound of the Voice of Revelation are in the world anew.

THE MESSENGER is the one chosen, prepared and sent into the world by the Angelic Assembly to receive the New Message from God. The Messenger for this time is Marshall Vian Summers. He is a humble man with no position in the world who has undergone a long and difficult preparation to be able to fulfill such an important role and mission in life. He is charged with a great burden, blessing and responsibility to receive God's pure Revelation and to protect and present it in the world. He is the first of God's Messengers to reveal the reality of a Greater Community of intelligent life in the universe. The Messenger has been engaged in a process of Revelation for over 30 years. He is alive in the world today.

THE SEAL OF THE PROPHETS is a seal established by God at the end of a Messenger's life. It seals the Revelation in purity, protecting against addition or alteration to God's communication. The Seal of the Prophets is established by God alone, and only God alone can break the Seal at those thresholds in humanity's evolution and emergence when God chooses to speak again.

THE PRESENCE can refer to the presence of Knowledge within the individual, the Presence of the Angelic Assembly and ultimately the Presence of God. The Presence of these three realities offers a life-changing experience of grace and relationship, which can be found by following the Mystery in life and by studying and practicing one of God's past Revelations or God's New Revelation for the world. The New Revelation offers a modern pathway to experiencing the power of this Presence in your life.

STEPS TO KNOWLEDGE is an ancient book of spiritual practice now being given by God to the world for the first time. In taking this mysterious journey, each person is led to the discovery of the power of Knowledge and the experience of profound inner knowing which can lead them to their higher purpose and calling in life.

THE GREATER COMMUNITY is the larger universe of intelligent life in which our world has always existed. This Greater Community encompasses all worlds in the universe where sentient life exists, in all states of evolution and development. The New Message reveals that humanity is in an early and adolescent phase of its development and that the time has now come for humanity to prepare to emerge into the Greater Community. It is here, standing at the threshold of space, that humanity discovers that it is not alone in the universe, or even within its own world.

THE GREATER DARKNESS is an Intervention underway by certain races from the Greater Community who are here to take advantage of a weak and divided humanity. This is occurring at a time when the human family is entering a period of increasing breakdown and disorder, in the face of the Great Waves of change. The Intervention presents itself as a benign and redeeming force while in reality its ultimate goal is to undermine human freedom and self-determination and take control of the world and its resources. The

New Message reveals that the Intervention seeks to secretly establish its influence here in the minds and hearts of people at a time of growing confusion, conflict and vulnerability. As the native peoples of this world, we are called upon to oppose this Intervention and to alert and educate others, thus uniting the human family in a great common purpose and preparing our world for the challenges and opportunities of life in the Greater Community.

THE GREAT WAVES OF CHANGE are a set of powerful environmental, economic and social forces now converging upon the world. The Great Waves are the result of humanity's misuse and overuse of the world, its resources and its environment. The Great Waves have the power to drastically alter the face of the world—producing economic instability, runaway climate change, violent weather and the loss of arable land and freshwater resources—threatening to produce a world condition of great difficulty and human suffering. The Great Waves are not an "end times" or apocalyptic event, but instead a period of transition to a new world condition. The New Message reveals what is coming for the world and the greater preparation that must be undertaken by enough people. It is calling for human unity and cooperation born now out of sheer necessity for the preservation and protection of human civilization.

HIGHER PURPOSE refers to the specific contribution each person was sent into the world to make and the unique relationships that will enable the fulfillment of this purpose. Knowledge within the individual holds their higher purpose and destiny for them. It cannot be ascertained by the intellect alone. It must be discovered, followed and expressed in service to others to be fully realized. The world needs the demonstration of this higher purpose from many more people as never before.

SPIRITUAL FAMILY refers to the small working groups formed after the Separation to enable all individuals to work towards greater states of union and relationship, undertaken over a long span of time, culminating in their final return to God. Your Spiritual Family represents the relationships you have reclaimed through Knowledge during your long journey through Separation. Some members of your Spiritual Family are in the world and some are beyond the world. The Spiritual Families are a part of the mysterious Plan of God to free and reunite all those living in Separation.

ANCIENT HOME refers to the reality of life and the state of awareness and relationship you had before entering the world, and to which you will return after your life in the world. Your Ancient Home is a state of connection and relationship with your Spiritual Family, the Assembly and God.

THE MESSENGER

Marshall Vian Summers is the Messenger for the New Message from God. For over three decades he has been the recipient of a vast New Revelation given to prepare humanity for the great economic, social and environmental change that is coming to the world and for humanity's emergence into a universe of intelligent life.

In the fall of 1981, at the age of 32, Marshall Vian Summers had a direct encounter with the Angelic Presence who had been guiding and preparing him for his future role and calling. This encounter forever altered the course of his existence and initiated him into a deeper relationship with the Angelic Assembly, requiring that he surrender his life to God.

Following this mysterious initiation, in the next few years to come he would receive the first revelations of the New Message from God. Over the decades since, a vast Revelation for humanity has unfolded, at times slowly and at times in great torrents. During these long years, he had to proceed with the support of only a few individuals, not knowing what this growing Revelation would mean and where it would ultimately lead. And so began the long, mysterious process of receiving God's New Message for humanity.

The Messenger has walked a long and difficult road to receive and present the largest Revelation ever given to the human family. Still today the Voice of Revelation continues to flow through him as he faces the great challenge of bringing God's New Revelation to a troubled and conflicted world.

Read and hear the Story of the Messenger:
newmessage.org/story

Hear and watch the world teachings of the Messenger:
newmessage.org/messenger

THE VOICE OF REVELATION

For the first time in history, you can hear the Voice of Revelation, such a Voice as spoke to the prophets and Messengers of the past, and is now speaking again through a new Messenger in the world today.

The Voice of Revelation is not the voice of one individual, but that of the entire Angelic Assembly speaking together, all as one. Here God communicates beyond words to the Angelic Assembly who then translate God's Message into human words and language that we can comprehend.

The revelations of this book were originally spoken in this manner by the Voice of Revelation, through the Messenger Marshall Vian Summers. This process of Divine Revelation has occurred since 1983. The Revelation continues to this day.

To hear the Voice of Revelation, which is the source of
the text contained in this book and throughout
the New Message, please visit
newmessage.org/experience.

Here the original audio recordings of the Voice
are made available to all people.

ABOUT THE WORLDWIDE COMMUNITY OF THE NEW MESSAGE FROM GOD

The New Message from God is being shared by people around the world. In more than 90 countries and in at least 23 languages, a Worldwide Community of students has formed to receive and study the New Message and support the mission of the Messenger and The Society.

Learn more about the worldwide community of people who are learning and living the New Message from God and taking the Steps to Knowledge towards a new and inspired life.

Become a part of a worldwide community of people who are pioneering a new chapter in the human experience. The New Message has the power to awaken the sleeping brilliance in people everywhere and bring new inspiration and wisdom into the lives of people from all nations and faith traditions.

Hear the Voice of Revelation speaking directly on the purpose and importance of the Worldwide Community:
newmessage.org/theworldwidecommunity

Learn more about the educational opportunities available in the Worldwide Community:

Forum - newmessage.org/forum
Free School - newmessage.org/school
Live Internet Broadcasts and International Events -
newmessage.org/events
Annual Encampment - newmessage.org/encampment
Online Library and Study Pathway - newmessage.org/experience

ABOUT THE SOCIETY FOR THE NEW MESSAGE

Founded in 1992 by Marshall Vian Summers, The Society for the New Message from God is an independent religious 501(c)(3) non-profit organization that is primarily supported by the students of the New Message, receiving no sponsorship or revenue from any government or religious organization.

The Society's mission is to bring the New Message from God to people everywhere so that humanity can find its common ground, preserve the Earth, protect human freedom and advance human civilization as we stand at the threshold of great change.

Marshall Vian Summers and The Society have been given the immense responsibility of bringing the New Message into the world. The members of The Society are a small group of dedicated individuals who have committed their lives to fulfill this mission. For them, it is a burden and a great blessing to give themselves wholeheartedly in this great service to humanity.

THE SOCIETY FOR THE NEW MESSAGE

Contact us:

P.O. Box 1724 Boulder, CO 80306-1724
(303) 938-8401
(800) 938-3891
011 303 938 84 01 (International)
(303) 938-1214 (fax)
society@newmessage.org
newmessage.org
alliesofhumanity.org
newknowledgelibrary.org

Connect with us:

youtube.com/thenewmessagefromgod
facebook.com/newmessagefromgod
facebook.com/marshallsummers
twitter.com/godsnewmessage

BOOKS OF THE NEW MESSAGE FROM GOD

God Has Spoken Again

Steps to Knowledge

Greater Community Spirituality

Relationships & Higher Purpose

Living The Way of Knowledge

Life in the Universe

The Great Waves of Change

Wisdom from the Greater Community I & II

Secrets of Heaven